Nelson Literacy

Senior Author
Jennette MacKenzie

Senior Consultant
Miriam P. Trehearne

Senior Consultant
Carmel Crévola

Series Consultants
Ruth McQuirter Scott—*Word Study*
Mary Reid—*Assessment*
Steven Reid—*Assessment*
James Coulter—*Assessment*
Neil Andersen—*Media*
Maureen Innes—*ESL/ELL*
Rod Peturson—*Science*
Maurice De Giuseppe—*Science*
Nancy Christoffer—*Bias and Equity*

Series Writing Team
Paula S. Goepfert, *Senior Writer*

Marg Camp	Wendy Mathieu
Kathleen Corrigan	Christine McClymont
James Coulter	Heather McGowan
Dianne Dillabough	Bev McMorris
Lalie Harcourt	Thérèse McNamara
Jane Hutchison	Sarah Peterson
Karen Kahler	Liz Powell
Norma Kennedy	Mary Schoones
Christel Kleitsch	Ricki Wortzman

NELSON EDUCATION

NELSON / EDUCATION

Nelson Literacy 3b
Jennette MacKenzie

Director of Publishing
Kevin Martindale

**General Manager,
Literacy and Reference**
Michelle Kelly

Director of Publishing, Literacy
Joe Banel

Publisher, Literacy
Rivka Cranley

**Managing Editor,
Development**
Lara Caplan

Senior Product Manager
Mark Cressman

Program Manager
Tracey MacDonald

Developmental Editors
Tara Harte
Norma Kennedy
David MacDonald

Researchers
Jane Hutchison
Dianne Dillabough

Assistant Editor
Adam Rennie

Editorial Assistants
Meghan Newton
Kendel Doyle

**Director, Content and Media
Production**
Carol Martin

Content Production Editor
Natalie Russell

Copy Editor
Linda Jenkins

Proofreader
Linda Szostak

Production Manager
Helen Locsin

Production Coordinator
Vicki Black

**Director, Asset Management
Services**
Vicki Gould

Design Director
Ken Phipps

Managing Designer
Sasha Moroz

Series Design
Sasha Moroz

Series Wordmark
Sasha Moroz

Cover Design
Sasha Moroz
Courtney Hellam

Interior Design
Carianne Bauldry
Jarrel Breckon
Nicole Dimson
Courtney Hellam
InContext Publishing Partners
Jennifer Laing
Jennifer Leung
Sasha Moroz
Jan John Rivera
Bill Smith Studio

Asset Coordinators
Suzanne Peden
Renée Ford

Compositor
Courtney Hellam

Photo Research and Permissions
Natalie Barrington

Printer
Transcontinental Printing

Advisers and Reviewers: Ontario

Nora Alexander

Stephanie Aubertin, Limestone DSB

Gale Bankowski, Hamilton-Wentworth CDSB

Wendy Bedford, Peterborough Victoria Northumberland and Clarington CDSB

Trudy Bell, Grand Erie DSB

Debra Boddy, Toronto DSB

Maggie Boss, Dufferin-Peel CDSB

Michelle Bryden, Eastern Ontario CDSB

Elizabeth M. Burchat, Renfrew CDSB

Karen Byromshaw, Toronto DSB

Mary Cairo, Toronto CDSB

Cheryl Chapman, Avon Maitland DSB

Cathy Chaput, Wellington CDSB

Christina Clancy, Dufferin-Peel CDSB

Alison Cooke, Grand Erie DSB

Sue Coutts, Simcoe County DSB

Cheryl Cristobal, Dufferin-Peel CDSB

Genevieve Dowson, Hamilton-Wentworth CDSB

Denise Edwards, Toronto DSB

Ted Gibb, Thames Valley DSB and University of Western Ontario

Lorraine Giroux, District School Board of Niagara

Charmaine Graves, Thames Valley DSB

Angela Harrison, York Region DSB

Colleen Hayward, Toronto CDSB

Charmaine Hung, Toronto DSB

Eddie Ing, Toronto DSB

Sue Jackson, Thames Valley DSB

Lee Jones-Imhotep, Toronto DSB

Ray King, Dufferin-Peel CDSB

Tanya Korostil, Peel DSB

Luci Lackey, Upper Grand DSB

Rocky Landon, Limestone DSB

Helen Lavigne, Waterloo CDSB

Laurie Light, Dufferin-Peel CDSB

Lorrie Lowes, Ottawa-Carleton DSB

Maria Makuch, Ottawa-Carleton DSB

Jennifer Mandarino, Dufferin-Peel CDSB

Carolyn March, Hamilton-Wentworth DSB

Mary Marshall, Halton DSB

Claire McDowell, Lambton Kent DSB

Thérèse McNamara, Simcoe County DSB

Andrew Mildenberger, Toronto DSB

Shirley Moorman, Simcoe County DSB

Laura Mossey, Durham DSB

Elisena Mycroft, Hamilton-Wentworth DSB

Mary Anne Olah, Toronto DSB

Judy Onody, Toronto CDSB

Eleanor Pardoe, Grand Erie DSB

Krista Pedersen, Upper Grand DSB

Sarah Peterson, Waterloo DSB

Annemarie Petrasek, Huron Perth CDSB

Catherine Pollock, Toronto DSB

Cheryl Potvin, Ottawa-Carleton DSB

Amarjit Rai, Peel DSB

Tara Rajaram-Donaldson, Toronto DSB

Mary Reid, Bluewater DSB

Kelly Rilley, Windsor-Essex CDSB

Joanne Saragosa, Toronto CDSB

Katherine Shaw, Peel DSB

Jackie Stafford, Toronto DSB

Elizabeth Taylor, Peel DSB

Sian Thomas, Renfrew DSB

Elizabeth Thompson, Durham DSB

Bonnie Tkac-Feetham, Niagara CDSB

Sandra VandeCamp, Dufferin-Peel CDSB

Ann Varty, Trillium Lakelands DSB

Contents

SOCIAL STUDIES

Welcome to
Nelson Literacy

Your *Nelson Literacy* book is full of fascinating stories and articles. Many of the topics are the same as those you will study in science and social studies.

Here are the different kinds of pages you will see in this book:

Let's Talk
Here's a chance to have some fun and also show what you know.

Understanding Strategies
These pages introduce you to reading, writing, speaking, listening, and media literacy strategies. Some pages have sticky notes with hints about the strategies.

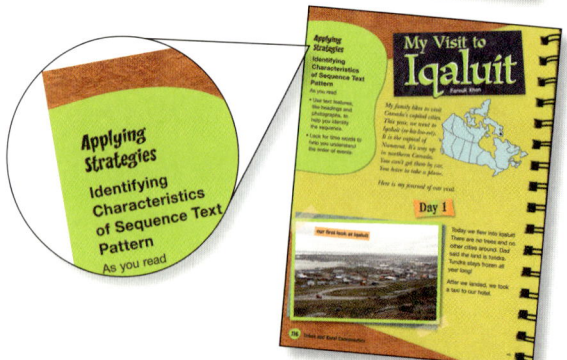

Applying Strategies
These pages give you the chance to try out the strategies you've learned.

Putting It All Together
At the end of each unit, you'll have the chance to use the strategies that you've learned.

Silly Stories

In this unit, you will

- identify characteristics of silly stories
- make inferences while you read
- identify conventions of comics
- find your personal voice
- make inferences while you listen

Spot the Silliness

What silly things can you find in this school cafeteria?
What makes them silly?

Narrative: Identifying Characteristics of Silly Stories

Silly stories have certain characteristics that make them silly:

- Strange or impossible things happen.

- The characters act as if nothing very strange is happening.

- The ending of the story makes readers smile.

GREEN CAT

Written and illustrated by Dayal Kaur Khalsa

Tom and Lynn shared a room.
They thought it was too small.
"I want more space!" each one would shout,
And try to toss the other out, into the drafty hall.

One night as they got set to fight,
A tall green cat stopped by.
He asked, "What do you like the most?"
Tom and Lynn responded, "Toast!"
He said, "Well, so do I."

↗

Strange or impossible things happen. What strange thing happens at the beginning of this story?

Green Cat went and got the toaster,
The kitchen table, chairs, a poster.
He said, "The best is yet to come,"
And brought two
    packages of gum.

The characters act as if nothing very strange is happening. How would you respond to a talking cat?

Napkins, plates, a spoon and honey,
A floor lamp, wall map, and—what's funny—
A bale of hay and a pig
    (though it wasn't very big).

Four flapping flags, nine napping cats,
Six silly geese in party hats.
A little leaning Tower of Pisa,
A potted palm, the Mona Lisa.

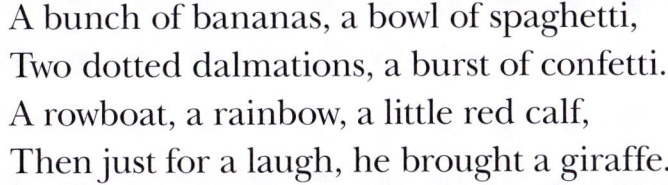

Strange or impossible things happen. Could these things happen in your house?

←

A bunch of bananas, a bowl of spaghetti,
Two dotted dalmations, a burst of confetti.
A rowboat, a rainbow, a little red calf,
Then just for a laugh, he brought a giraffe.

From a corner of the clutter,
Tom and Lynn were heard to mutter,
In voices muffled dim as doom,
"We … need … more … room!"

Strange or impossible things happen. How well would a rowboat and a rainbow fit in your room?

←

Out went the tower, the bananas, confetti,
Dalmations, the picture, the palm, the spaghetti,
The geese and the rowboat, the flags and the cats,
The pig and the hay and the rainbow and hats,

The floor lamp, the wall map, the spoon and the toaster,
The plates and the napkins, the table, the poster,
The chairs and the honey, the bread, gum, and calf,
And finally Green Cat took away the giraffe.

The characters act as if nothing very strange is happening. How would you answer Green Cat?

→

Often the ending of the story makes readers smile. What do you think of Tom and Lynn's solution to the problem of "too much room"?

→

"Enough room now?" Green Cat asked.
"Yes, yes!" said Tom and Lynn.
He hugged them both with all his might,
Turned off the light and said, "Good night,
Until we meet again."

They lay upon their little beds,
    but sleep did not come soon.
They tossed and turned for half the night.
Said Tom, "The room does not feel right."
Said Lynn, "There's too much room."

And so they tiptoed down the stairs,
And brought back up the kitchen chairs.

The Best Worst Birthday Ever

Written by Diane Robitaille   Illustrated by Mike Laughhead

Then, the circus ponies were grumpy. They wouldn't do any tricks until we gave them some cake. Then they complained because it wasn't chocolate!

OPEN MY PRESENT FIRST!

WHERE'S THE CAKE?

Next, the giraffe and elephant got away. I didn't mind, because they had been eating all the snacks. I did mind when I saw that they took the loot bags with them!

HEY, THERE GO THE LOOT BAGS!

It's going to take *forever* to clean up this mess! At least all my friends said they had a ton of fun.

FOR MY BIRTHDAY NEXT YEAR, I'VE INVITED THE ZOO. I HOPE YOU LIKE SNAKES, DAD!

Reflect on

Strategies: How does this story match the characteristics of silly stories? Find three examples.

Connections: What kind of a birthday party would you have if you could turn your party into a silly story?

Mrs. Murphy, and Mrs. Murphy's Kids

Written by Dennis Lee

Illustrated by Scott Burroughs

Applying Strategies

Narrative: Identifying Characteristics of Silly Stories

As you read, look for these characteristics of silly stories:

- Strange or impossible things happen.
- The characters act as if nothing very strange is happening.
- The ending of the story makes readers smile.

Mrs. Murphy,
    If you please,
Kept her kids
    In a can of peas.

The kids got bigger
    And the can filled up,
So she moved them into
    A measuring cup.

But the kids got bigger
    And the cup got crammed,
So she poured them into
    A frying pan.

But the kids grew bigger
    And the pan began to stink,
So she pitched them all
    In the kitchen sink.

But the kids kept growing
　　And the sink went *kaplooey*,
So she dumped them on their ears
　　In a crate of chop suey.

But the kids kept growing
　　And the crate got stuck,
So she carted them away
　　In a ten-tonne truck.

And she said, "Thank goodness
　　I remembered that truck,
Or my poor little children
　　Would be out of luck!"

But the darn kids grew
　　Till the truck wouldn't fit,
And she had to haul them off
　　To a gravel pit.

But the kids kept growing
　　Till the pit was too small,
So she bedded them down
　　In a shopping mall.

But the kids grew enormous
    And the mall wouldn't do,
So she herded them together
    In an empty zoo.

But the kids grew gigantic
    And the fence went *pop*!
So she towed them away
    To a mountain top.

But the kids just grew
    And the mountain broke apart,
And she said, "Darned kids,
    They were pesky from the start!"

So she waited for a year,
    And she waited for another,
And the kids grew up
    And had babies like their mother.

And Mrs. Murphy's kids—
    You can think what you please—
Kept all *their* kids
    In a can of peas.

SINCE
YUMMY'S

Sweet Peas

Reflect on

Strategies: How does this poem match the characteristics of silly stories? Find three examples.

Critical Literacy: How would this poem be different if it were told from the point of view of Mrs. Murphy's kids?

17

Identifying Conventions of Comics

Funny!

The comics section in the newspaper used to be called "the funnies" because comics make people laugh. Every comic tells a joke. How do they do it?

A comic is a joke divided into sections called panels. What is happening in the first panel of this comic?

The illustration is part of the joke. What does the cartoonist do to make the comic funny?

Speech balloons show what characters say. Thought balloons show what characters think. Which words in this comic are spoken? Which words are someone's thoughts?

The last panel makes you laugh. How does this comic end? Why does it make you laugh?

Have fun reading this comic! How does the cartoonist
use illustrations to tell the joke? Why does the last
panel make you laugh?

Making Inferences

Making inferences is sometimes called "reading between the lines." An author may not tell you everything. You can use what you already know and clues from the text to make inferences.

↗

Connect to what you already know. How do you think Patrick feels about sleeping over at his Granny's house for the first time?

↗

Use clues from the text and illustrations to read between the lines. Do you think Patrick will get to bed soon?

WHAT!

Written by Kate Lum
Illustrated by Adrian Johnson

Once upon a time there was a boy named Patrick who was having his first sleepover at his Granny's house.

As the sun began to set, Granny said, "Patrick, dear boy! Time to get ready for bed."

"But Granny," said Patrick. "I don't HAVE a bed here."

"WHAT?" cried Granny. She ran out to her yard where some tall trees were growing, and chopped one down.

She carried it to her workroom, and made Patrick a fine bed.

Then she painted it a restful shade of blue, put a mattress on it, and took it to the bedroom.

CRIED GRANNY

"There you are, dear boy," said Granny. "Now climb into bed, lay your head on the pillow, and sail off to Dreamland!"

"But Granny," said Patrick. "I don't HAVE a pillow here!"

"WHAT?!?" cried Granny. She ran out to her henhouse, woke up the chickens, and collected a big batch of feathers.

She took them to her sewing room where she made a bag out of cloth. Then she stuffed it with the feathers, sewed it up neatly, and gave it to Patrick.

"There you are, dear boy," said Granny. "Now climb into bed, lay your head on the pillow, tuck the blanket under your chin, and I'll kiss you good night."

"But Granny," said Patrick. "I don't HAVE a blanket here!"

Use clues from the text and illustrations to read between the lines. How does Granny feel about Patrick going to bed?

→

→

Use clues from the text and illustrations to read between the lines. Did Patrick enjoy his sleepover? Did Granny enjoy the sleepover?

"WHAAAT??!!??" cried Granny. She ran outside and headed for the hills where a flock of fat sheep were snoozing. She sheared off some of their wool and ran right back home.

She spun the wool into yarn, knitted a fuzzy warm blanket, and dyed it twilight purple. When it was dry, she carried it upstairs and spread it on the bed.

"NOW, PATRICK!" cried Granny. "CLIMB into bed. LAY your head on the pillow. TUCK the blanket under your chin. And …
GO TO SLEEP!"

"But Granny," said Patrick. "It's morning."

"WHAAAAAAAT!!!!" cried Granny.

HE CAME WITH THE COUCH

Written and illustrated by David Slonim

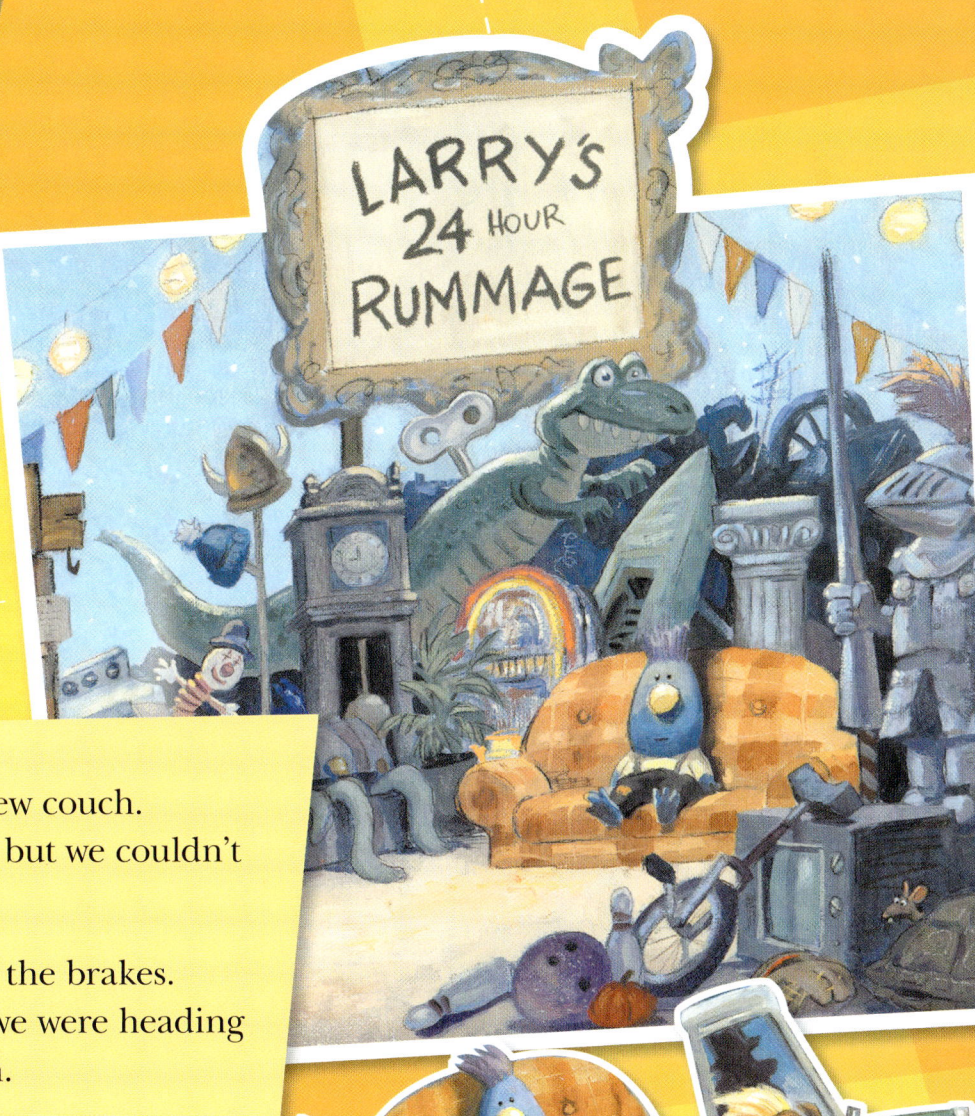

Our family needed a new couch. We looked and looked, but we couldn't find a couch we liked.

Then Dad suddenly hit the brakes. "Aha!" he cried. Soon we were heading home with a new couch.

"Who is that back there?" I asked. "I don't know," said Dad. "He came with the couch."

NEL

The next morning he was still there.
So I gave him some toast.

"I'm Sophie," I told him.
"Who are you?"
But he didn't say anything.

"Can we keep him?" I asked.
"No," said Dad.

Mom and Dad tried to get him
to leave. But he didn't budge.
"Maybe he's sick," I said.
So they called the doctor.

The doctor said, "He needs to get out more."

So we took him to the mountains. We took him to the beach. We took him to the CN Tower. But he never left the couch.

Mom and Dad said we'd just have to get used to him. "Great!" I said.

Then one day a branch snapped
and I fell from my tree.
"Help!" I screamed.
There was a sudden crash.
He saved me!

That's why we're all so glad he came
with the couch.

But it wasn't long before we were off
to another rummage sale.
She came with the chair!

Reflect on

Strategies: How did using clues from the text and illustrations help you to read between the lines?

Connections: How would your family react if "he" came with your couch?

NEL

Amos's Sweater

Written by Janet Lunn
Illustrated by Kim LaFave

Applying Strategies

Making Inferences

As you read, make inferences to help you understand what you are reading:

- Connect to what you already know.

- Use clues from the text and illustrations to read between the lines.

- Think about what a character's actions tell you about that character's personality.

Amos was old and Amos was cold and Amos was tired of giving away all his wool.

So one summer day when Aunt Hattie went out to the pasture with her big clipping shears, Amos balked.

"Baa," he cried. He butted Aunt Hattie. And ran away.

"Amos, stop!" shouted Aunt Hattie. "Stop, Amos!" But Amos did not stop.

Aunt Hattie ran after him. She chased him around the meadow. She chased him up and down the hillside and across the brook.

But Amos was too fast.

Uncle Henry had to help catch him and hold him down.

Then Aunt Hattie clipped his wool.

"There, now, Amos," she said. "That wasn't so bad, was it?"

"Baa," said Amos.

Aunt Hattie gave him an apple to make him feel better. But Amos did not feel better. He was old and he was cold and now he was angry.

Aunt Hattie washed the wool. She combed it and she spun it. Then she knitted the wool into a big, warm sweater for Uncle Henry.

"Isn't that fine, Amos?" She showed him the big, warm sweater.

"Baa." Amos snatched at the sweater with his teeth.

NEL

Every time Amos saw Uncle Henry wearing his sweater, he bit it. There were always 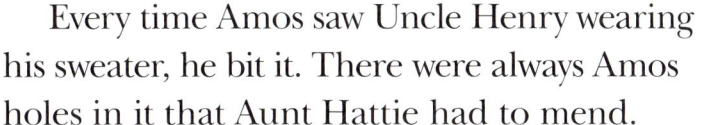 Amos holes in it that Aunt Hattie had to mend.

One hot day, when Uncle Henry left the sweater over the fence, Amos tried to pull it down. It stuck fast and he made such a huge hole in it, Aunt Hattie came after him with a stick.

Aunt Hattie mended the huge hole. She washed the sweater and hung it out to dry. Amos waited for her to go back into the house.

Then he made a jump for it. But the line was too high.

One night, Uncle Henry left the sweater on the table in the back kitchen of the house. The door was open. The moon was full. Amos could see the sweater from his stall in the barn.

He butted the stall door. He shoved it. He butted it. He shoved it. He butted and shoved until the door flew open.

He dashed across the barnyard into the back kitchen. He yanked the sweater off the table. Furiously, he pulled it this way and that. An end of yarn caught in his hoof.

He pulled and he twisted to get it loose. He tugged. He twisted. He bit. He rolled around on the floor. The more he struggled the tighter the yarn wound around him.

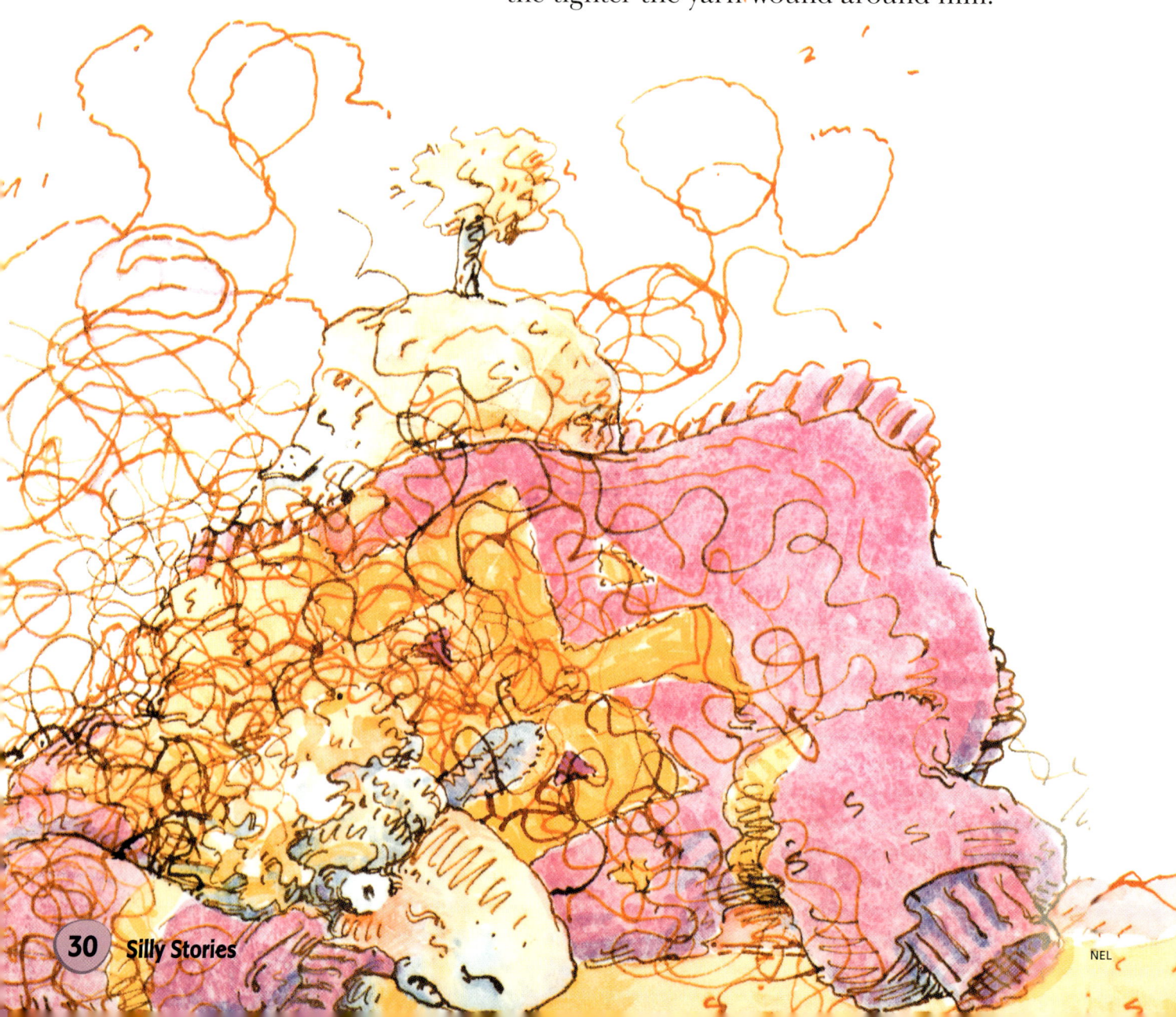

Soon he was so tangled you couldn't tell which was yarn, which was sweater, which was Amos.

"Baa," he cried,"Baa, baaaa," in such rage that Aunt Hattie and Uncle Henry came running to see what had happened.

"Oh, Amos. Now you've done it!"

Aunt Hattie sighed. Uncle Henry laughed. He began to unwind the yarn. Amos glared at them with his angry black eyes.

Free at last, he stood up. His two front legs were deep in the arms of Uncle Henry's sweater. His head poked through the top.

NEL

"You know, Hattie, Amos is old," said Uncle Henry.

"And maybe Amos is cold," said Aunt Hattie.

"And maybe," they both said, "Amos is tired of giving away all his wool."

Now, if you go by the farm where Aunt Hattie and Uncle Henry live, you will see the sheep out in the pasture. There is one, standing a little apart. That is Amos.

He is old. But he is not cold because he is wearing his sweater.

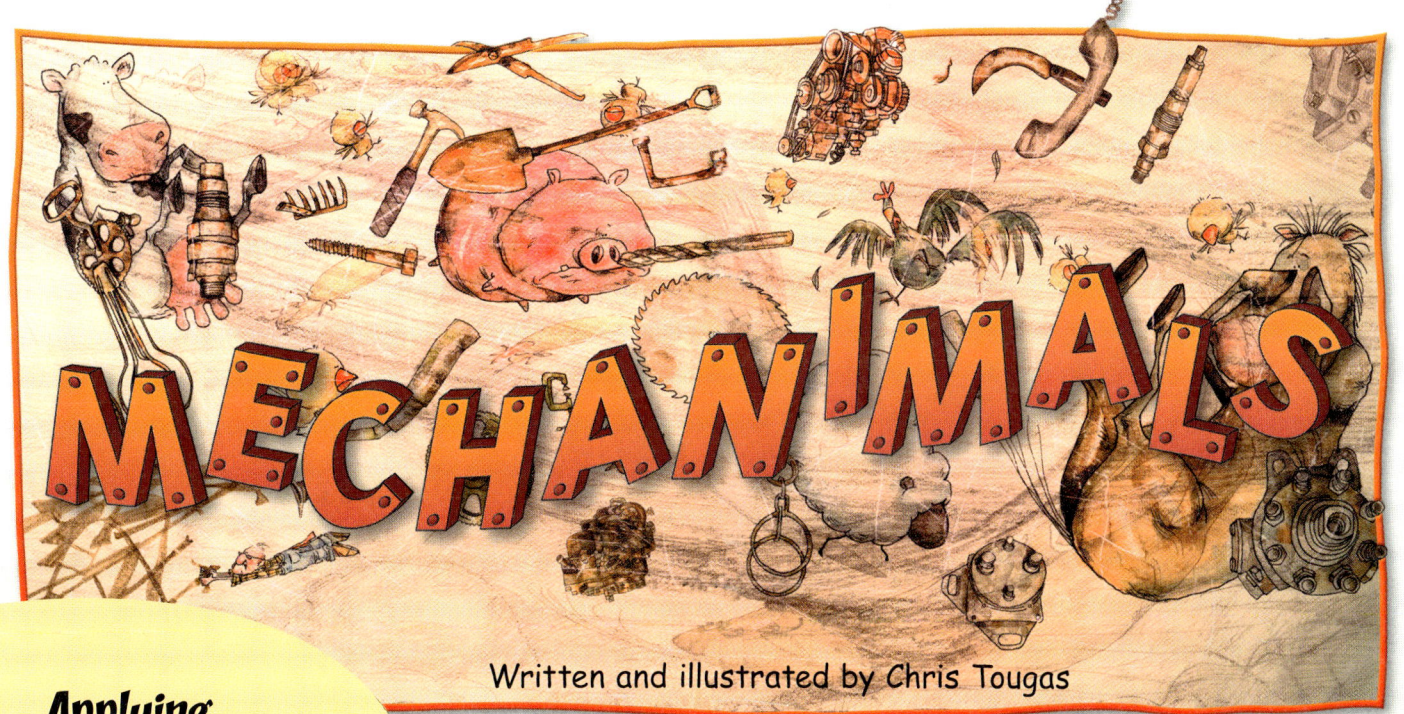

MECHANIMALS

Written and illustrated by Chris Tougas

There once was a farmer who had lots of animals that got swept away by a tornado.

The twister left behind a mountain of scrap metal and machine parts … and a very sad farmer.

Determined not to give up, the farmer declared, "I'll turn this mess into a masterpiece."

"When pigs fly," his neighbours replied, which gave him an idea.

There was much to be done. First he had to get organized. Then he had to draw up his plans. At last it was time to get to work.

First the farmer made a rooster-bot so he wouldn't sleep in too late. It was so loud, it woke people in China.

Next he made a bunch of chick-bots to help with all the heavy lifting. They were incredibly strong.

The cow-bot helped with all the lube and fuelling. She also made great chocolate milk.

The sheep-bot had a coat of steel wool to help the farmer buff all the metal.

Of course he needed a horse-bot to help him haul in the lunch. Holy horsepower!

Those mechanimals sure loved munching on metal.

Finally, he needed a flying pig-bot to zip around the farm. And now when people say, "When pigs fly!"

… they really mean it!

Reflect on

Strategies: How did connecting to what you already know help you make inferences?

Critical Literacy: How do you think the author feels about recycling? How do you know?

Finding Your Personal Voice

The personality you know best is your own. You can make your writing enjoyable by putting your personal voice into it.

These two students brainstormed ideas for a silly story. They both liked the idea of a talking baseball. Notice how their personal voices make the beginnings of the two stories different and enjoyable.

THE TALKING BASEBALL
By Serena
The smooth, round ball felt at home in Holly's hand. She looked out over the emerald-green grass and raised her arm to throw. That's when the ball said, "I think you need to adjust your aim."

THE TALKING BASEBALL
By Olivia
Baseball is my game. You know how it feels to smack that ball, right? Well, so do I! But as my bat whipped around, I heard a squeaky voice coming at me. "Don't hit me, you maniac!" screeched the ball.

How to find your personal voice:

- ✔ **Put yourself inside your story.** Ask yourself, "How do I feel?"

- ✔ **Think about how you talk.** Ask yourself, "How would I tell this story if I were talking?"

- ✔ **Write a few sentences.** Ask yourself, "Does this sound like me?"

**Reading Like
a Writer**

As you read, identify
the personal voice
in the story. Think
about how the author
uses a personal
voice to make the
story enjoyable.

The Day Jimmy's Boa Ate the Wash

Written by Trinka Hakes Noble
Illustrated by Steven Kellogg

"How was your class trip to the farm?"

"Oh … boring … kind of dull … until the cow started crying."

"A cow … crying?"

"Yeah, you see, a haystack fell on her."

"But a haystack doesn't just fall over."

"It does if a farmer crashes into it with his tractor."

"Oh, come on, a farmer wouldn't do that."

"He would if he were too busy yelling at the pigs to get off our school bus."

"What were the pigs doing on the bus?"

"Eating our lunches."

"Why were they eating your lunches?"

"Because we threw their corn at each other, and they didn't have anything else to eat."

"Well, that makes sense, but why were you throwing corn?"

"Because we ran out of eggs."

"Out of eggs? Why were you throwing eggs?"

"Because of the boa constrictor."

"THE BOA CONSTRICTOR!"

"Yeah, Jimmy's pet boa constrictor."

"What was Jimmy's pet boa constrictor doing on the farm?"

"Oh, he brought it to meet all the farm animals, but the chickens didn't like it."

"You mean he took it into the hen house?"

"Yeah, and the chickens started squawking and flying around."

"Go on, go on. What happened?"

"Well, one hen got excited and laid an egg, and it landed on Jenny's head."

"The hen?"

"No, the egg. And it broke—yucky—all over her hair."

"What did she do?"

"She got mad because she thought Tommy threw it, so she threw one at him."

"What did Tommy do?"

"Oh, he ducked and the egg hit Marianne in the face. So she threw one at Jenny but she missed and hit Jimmy, who dropped his boa constrictor."

"Oh, and I know, the next thing you knew, everyone was throwing eggs, right?"

"Right."

"And when you ran out of eggs, you threw the pigs' corn, right?"

"Right again."

"Well, what finally stopped it?"

"Well, we heard the farmer's wife screaming."

"Why was she screaming?"

"We never found out, because Mrs. Stanley made us get on the bus, and we sort of left in a hurry without the boa constrictor."

"I bet Jimmy was sad because he left his pet boa constrictor."

"Oh, not really. We left in such a hurry that one of the pigs didn't get off the bus, so now he's got a pet pig."

"Boy, that sure sounds like an exciting trip."

"Yeah, I suppose, if you're the kind of kid who likes class trips to the farm."

Reflect on

Writer's Craft: How does the author's voice make this story enjoyable? Give examples from the story to help explain your ideas.

Connections: How are your feelings about class trips like the author's feelings? How are they different?

Understanding **listening** strategies

Making Inferences While You Listen

Making inferences while you listen can help you become an active listener.

TWO POEMS.

PERFORMED BY SAMUEL AND ANWAR.

THIS IS GOING TO BE FUNNY. THESE GUYS ARE NEVER SERIOUS!

THE FIRST POEM

AS I WAS STANDING IN THE STREET, AS QUIET AS CAN BE,

A GREAT BIG UGLY MAN CAME UP AND TIED HIS HORSE TO ME.

THEY PROBABLY READ A LOT OF POEMS.

I KNOW THEY PRACTISED THAT! THEY'RE HILARIOUS.

THE SECOND POEM

I EAT MY PEAS WITH HONEY. I'VE DONE IT ALL MY LIFE,

THEY DO TASTE KIND OF FUNNY, BUT IT KEEPS THEM ON THE KNIFE.

I BET THEY TRIED PEAS WITH HONEY!

THEY LOOK LIKE THEY'RE HAVING FUN!

How to make inferences while you listen:

☑ Connect to what you already know.

☑ Watch the speaker's face and gestures.

☑ Listen to the tone and speed of the speaker's voice.

☑ Listen for clues in what the speaker says.

Jeffrey and Sloth

Written by Kari-Lynn Winters • Illustrated by Ben Hodson

Jeffrey looked at the blank page. It glared back.

He tried to write but couldn't think of something to write about. So he doodled instead.

He found himself sketching a round-bellied, long-armed sloth.

"Focus on the words," Jeffrey muttered.

"Forget about the words," whispered a voice.

Jeffrey looked around, his eyes wide. "Who said that?"

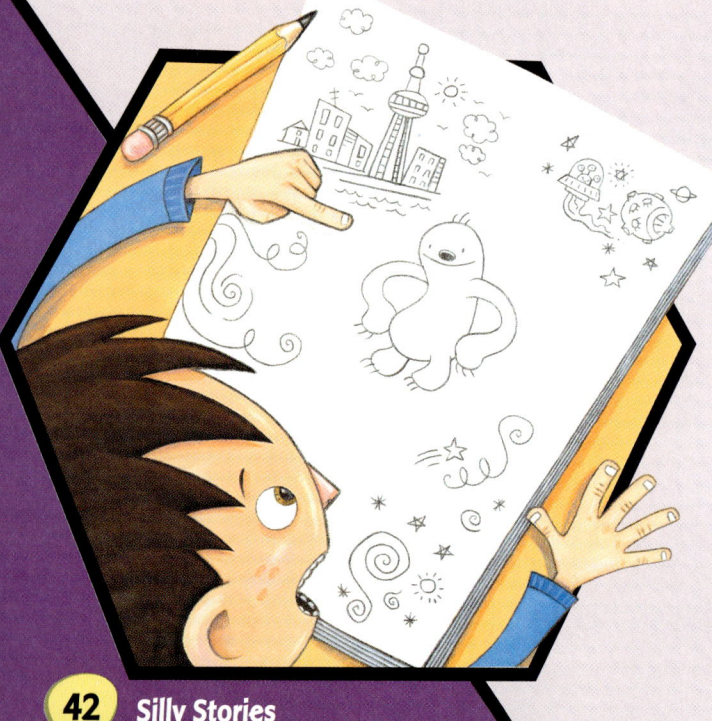

Down on the page, the sloth he had sketched looked different. "Hey, I didn't draw you with your hands on your hips!" Jeffrey said.

"Good writers have lots of ideas," declared Sloth. "*You* don't have any! You should stick to drawing."

"W-w-what d-do you know anyway?" Jeffrey stammered.

"I know you're a lousy writer," said Sloth.

"I am not a lousy writer! I just can't think of anything to write about."

"Well, instead of drawing the CN Tower, make yourself useful and sketch me a chair."

Sloth pointed at a spot on the page.

Jeffrey sat down and did as he was told.

Sloth relaxed into the chair. "Nice, but a pillow would make it even better. Draw me a puffy pillow."

Jeffrey drew a pillow.

"Now sketch me a cozy blanket."

"I'll never finish my homework at this rate!" Jeffrey said.

"You're right," Sloth laughed. "It *is* taking forever. So do something you're good at and draw me a blanket."

Jeffrey was tired of listening to Sloth. He began to write.

Once there was a pudgy sloth who searched for the world's coziest blanket.

"Who are you calling pudgy?" Sloth said. Jeffrey ignored Sloth and went on writing.

He looked up high for that blanket.

Sloth looked to the sky.

He looked down low for that blanket.

Sloth peeked under the chair. "I sure would like that blanket."

Jeffrey now realized what was happening. "I get it. You don't want me to write because you're lazy."

"That's not it," Sloth said.

"Oh yeah? So if I wrote a story making you dig clear through the Earth, you wouldn't care?"

Sloth looked worried. "Absolutely not."

"And if I wrote about you swimming across the ocean, you'd be happy?"

Sloth was sweating now. "I might be happy."

"What if I made you search all of Canada for a cozy—"

Sloth interrupted. "If I could find that cozy blanket, I wouldn't mind."

"Canada is a big place. You'd have to climb mountains, trek across the tundra, paddle the Great Lakes, and hike the Prairies."

"You can't make me!"

"Oh yeah?" Jeffrey said.

He picked up his pencil, sketched a shovel, and continued his story.

He began to dig.

Sloth had no choice but to dig.

He dug a hole clear through the Earth to India.

"I need some water. Quick, write about water," ordered Sloth.

Then he swam to France. He really wanted to find the world's coziest blanket.

"That's not what I meant!" said Sloth.

But the coziest blanket wasn't there.

Now Jeffrey was smiling.

He would have to search all of Canada. He climbed, trekked, paddled, hiked, stumbled along...

"I'm afraid that I made a great mistake." Sloth was panting. He was not used to so much exercise. "I said that your writing was lousy," Sloth huffed. "I should have said that your writing is very engaging. And that it makes a lot of sense. Honestly, I mean that. You're a good ... no, a great ... no, a marvellous writ—"

"Okay," said Jeffrey.

He looked down at the page.

"Yes!" he cheered. Thanks to Sloth, his homework was done! Jeffrey beamed as he sketched a blanket and wrote:

And finally, the very tired sloth found the world's coziest blanket, wrapped himself up in it and fell fast asleep ... at least for that evening.

Reflect on

Strategies: How did using the strategies you learned in this unit help you enjoy the story?

Your Learning: What ideas did this story give you about how to get started on a piece of writing?

Forces Causing Movement

In this unit, you will

- ask questions as you read
- ask questions when you listen
- write with a strong voice
- recognize different points of view
- learn about forces causing movement
- use photos and captions

A Day at the Park

In this picture, find at least three things that are being pushed and three things that are being pulled. Can you find more?

Questioning

Asking questions makes you an active reader and helps you understand what you are reading.

Move It!

Written by Adrienne Mason
Illustrated by Anton Petrov

→

Ask questions to check your understanding. Does this make sense? When do you use force?

Push and Pull

You use pushes and pulls to make things move. A push moves an object away. A pull brings it closer. A push or pull is called a *force*.

On the Move

You use force to move your body. To walk, you push against the ground. You also use force to move things. You pull a wagon to make it move.

How are these children using force to move their bodies or other things?

Make It Move

Things do not start moving unless they are pushed or pulled. When you lift something, you are pulling it up. When you throw something, you are pushing it away.

How are the children above using pushes or pulls to make things move?

Ask questions about things you wonder about. Do you use more force when you throw a ball a long distance than you do when you throw it a short distance?

←

Get Moving!

A force is a push or pull that starts an object moving or changes its motion.

→

Ask questions to check your understanding. Does this make sense? How do you use force when you are doing schoolwork?

A force can start an object moving.

A force can stop a moving object.

A force can change the direction of an object that is already moving.

Stop It!

To stop something that is moving, you need to use force. You stop a ball by pushing in the opposite direction.

The faster something moves, the more force it takes to stop it.

Down to Earth

If you throw something up, it will fall back down. It is pulled down by a force called *gravity*.

You can't see gravity, but it pulls things—including you—down toward Earth. This is why things fall to the ground when you drop them.

Slow Motion

You push on the pedals to make your bicycle move. When you stop pushing, your bicycle slows down and stops. Why?

Your bicycle tires are rubbing against the road. When two surfaces rub together, there is a force called *friction*.

Friction makes moving things slow down and then stop. Friction also helps you grip the ground when you walk or run.

Ask questions to connect to what you know. Why is it easier to run on the sidewalk than on ice?

GRAVITY IS GREAT

Written by Linda Corso
Illustrated by Ron Berg

Where do things go when they fall? Down, down, down!

Things fall because there is gravity. Gravity is a force that pulls things down.

Gravity also pulls on things that are not falling. Rugs and chairs stay on the floor. That is because gravity is always pulling down on them.

What would life be like if we did not have gravity?

Basketball would not be any fun. The ball would not fall down into the hoop.

You would not be able to go down a slide. You need gravity to pull you down.

Gravity pulls rain down from the sky.

Gravity pulls you down after you jump up.

Gravity makes coins drop down into your piggy bank.

Gravity pulls down on everything!

Reflect on

Strategies: Find a place where asking a question helped you understand what you were reading.

Connections: How does gravity help you have fun?

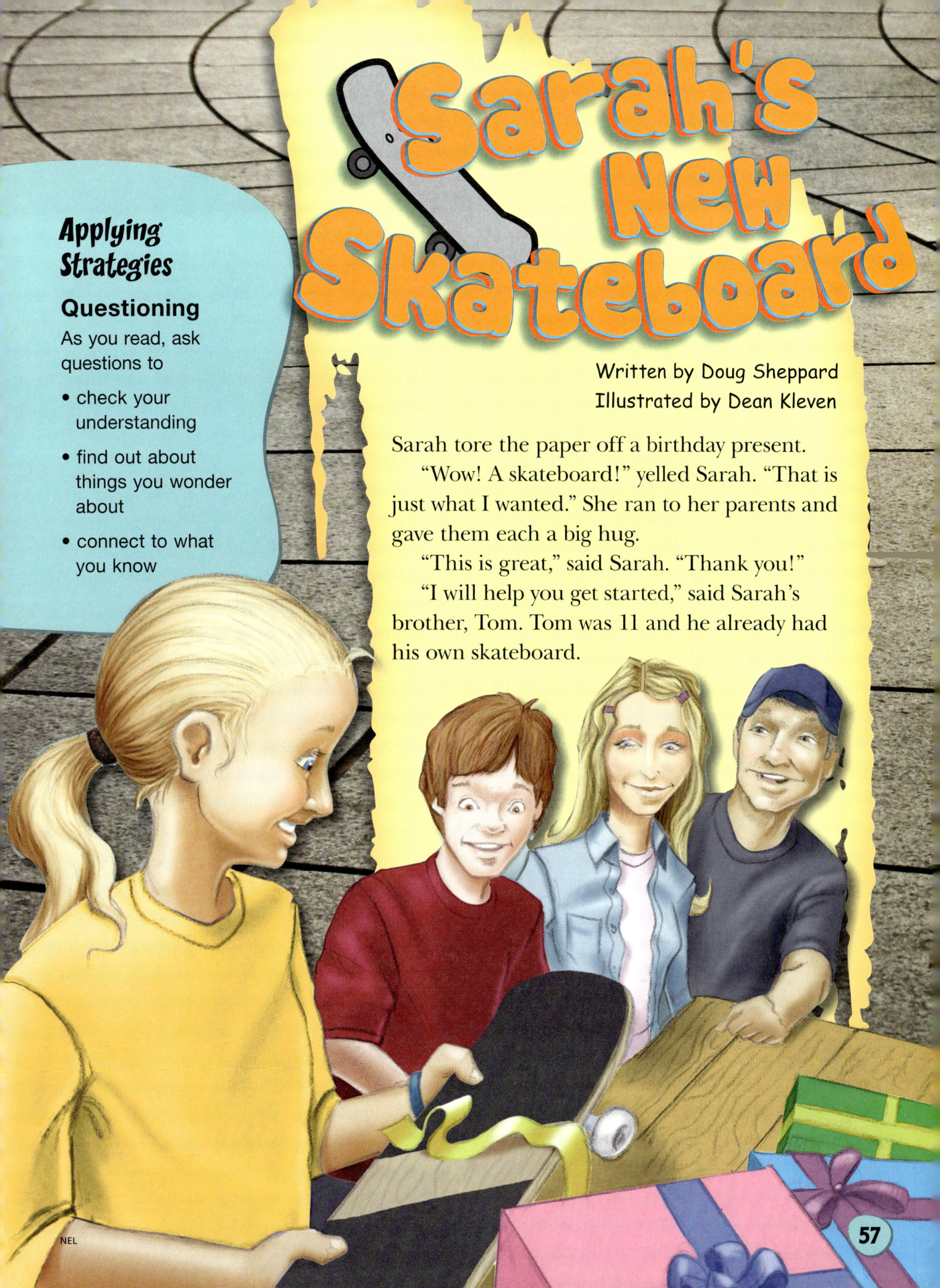

Sarah's New Skateboard

Written by Doug Sheppard
Illustrated by Dean Kleven

Applying Strategies

Questioning

As you read, ask questions to

- check your understanding
- find out about things you wonder about
- connect to what you know

Sarah tore the paper off a birthday present.

"Wow! A skateboard!" yelled Sarah. "That is just what I wanted." She ran to her parents and gave them each a big hug.

"This is great," said Sarah. "Thank you!"

"I will help you get started," said Sarah's brother, Tom. Tom was 11 and he already had his own skateboard.

Sarah and Tom went out to the driveway. "How do I start?" asked Sarah.

"To get moving, you push off with one foot," said Tom. Sarah gave it a try. She rolled along the driveway.

"Hey! How do I stop?" called Sarah. "Where are the brakes?"

"Push down with your back foot," called Tom. "The end of the board will drag on the ground. That will make you stop."

Sarah tried it. She almost fell when the skateboard tilted up, but soon she stopped.

"It worked!" she said.

"It works because of friction," said Tom.

"What is friction?" asked Sarah.

"Friction is a force that happens when things rub together," said Tom. "Friction makes things slow down and then stop."

"So the skateboard makes friction when the back end drags on the ground," said Sarah.

"Right," said Tom.

"Now can you teach me some skateboard tricks?" asked Sarah.

Tom smiled. "You are just getting started," he said. "Let's try stopping a few more times."

Sarah loved her new skateboard. It was her best birthday present ever.

Reflect on

Strategies: Did you ask questions to connect to what you know? How did this help you understand the story?

Your Learning: What can you tell skateboarders about how forces help them enjoy this sport?

What Can Magnets Do?

Magnets Push and Pull

Magnets come in many shapes and sizes. Some magnets are flat and straight. Others are curved or round. All magnets can push or pull some objects. Pushes and pulls are forces.

Bar Magnet

Magnets Have Poles

All magnets have two poles. A pole is the place on a magnet where the force is the strongest. The poles are in different places on different magnets. On a bar magnet, one pole is labelled N for north pole. The other pole is labelled S for south pole.

Ring Magnet

N ↓   S ↓

Magnets Act on Each Other

All magnets have forces that act on other magnets. The force between two magnets can be either a push or a pull.

If the north pole of one magnet is near the south pole of another magnet, the magnets attract. When a magnet attracts another magnet, it pulls the other magnet toward itself. Unlike poles attract each other.

If two north poles are near each other or two south poles are near each other, the magnets repel. When a magnet repels another magnet, it pushes the other magnet away from itself. Like poles repel each other.

Unlike poles attract

Like poles repel

Like poles repel

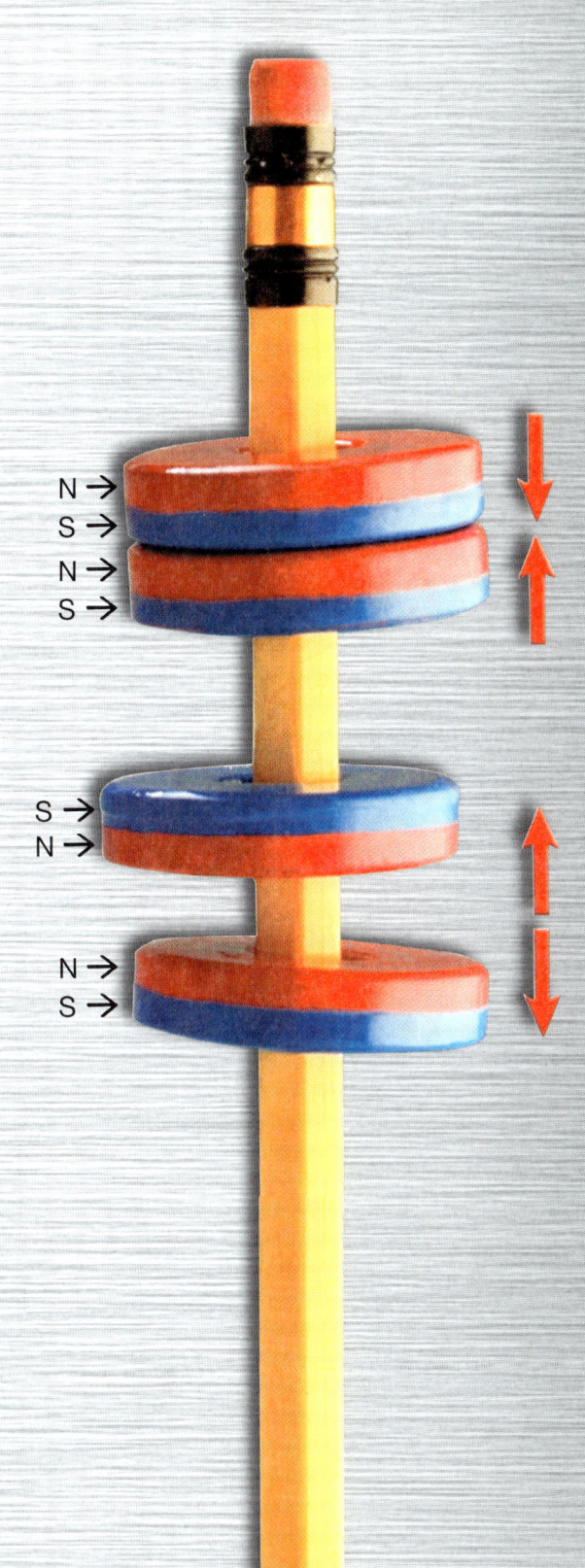

Objects That Magnets Attract

You have learned that magnets can attract other magnets. Magnets can attract other objects, too. Magnets can attract objects that have a metal called iron in them.

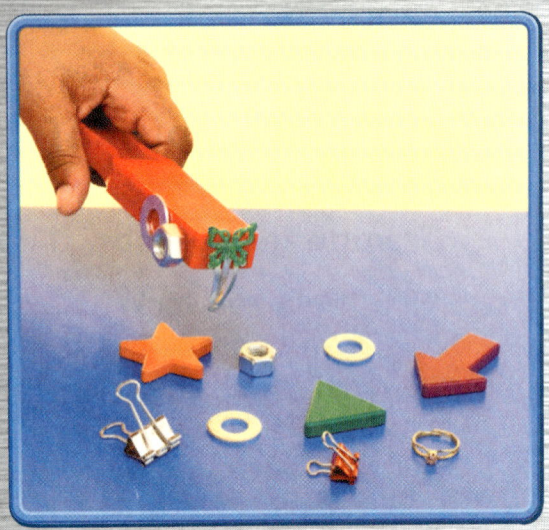

A magnet attracts objects that have iron in them.

Objects That Are Not Attracted by Magnets

Some objects are not attracted by magnets. Objects that are made from glass, paper, wood, or plastic are not attracted by magnets.

Everyday Magnets

Many common objects use magnetic force to help them work. Some computer games have magnets inside. Some toy cars use magnets to make their motors run. Magnets help keep refrigerator doors closed.

A magnet does not attract plastic animals.

Try an Experiment!

Try this experiment to learn about a magnet's force.

What You Need

- magnet
- paper clip on a string
- tape
- test objects: squares of paper, cardboard, foil, and plastic

What You Do

Step 1 Hang a paper clip from a table edge with string and tape.

Step 2 Wave a magnet under the clip. Watch what happens to the clip.

Step 3 Have a partner slide an object between the magnet and the clip. Wave the magnet again. Test the other objects.

Step 4 Watch what happens to the clip.

Think and Share

1. Which objects did the magnet's force pass through?

2. What other objects do you think the magnet's force will pass through? Tell why you think so.

Reflect on

Strategies: How did asking questions help you understand how magnets work?

Critical Literacy: How can you tell the author thinks it's important to understand how magnets work?

Making Voice Strong

Voice is what gives writing power. When writing has a strong voice, readers feel like they can "hear" how excited you are about your writing.

This writer used interesting words to make the voice in her report stronger.

Forces make soccer fun
~~Forces are important in soccer.~~ When my foot ~~hits~~ smacks the ball, I am using force. The ball ~~goes~~ sails through the air. Another player can use force to stop the ball. I ~~like it best~~ cheer when the other team's net stops the ball. ~~Then we have a goal.~~ We score!

How to make voice strong:

☑ Imagine you are talking instead of writing. Think about how you show your excitement.

☑ Read your writing out loud.

☑ Make your voice stronger by changing boring words to interesting words.

FORCE DETECTIVE

Written by Norma Kennedy
Illustrated by Matt Roussel

"Dad! I'm home!" I shouted.

"Hi, Gumdrop. How was school?" Dad asked as he gave me a huge hug.

My dad calls me Gumdrop. Everyone else calls me Flora. That's my real name.

"Okay, I guess. Ms. Pastin gave us homework. I have to find some examples of forces," I said.

Dad asked, "Have you thought of any?"

"Just that Ms. Pastin is *forcing* us to do this homework," I joked.

"Hey, that's pretty funny, Gumdrop. I'll leave you alone. That will *force* you to think harder. Ha ha." Dad laughed at his own joke.

I rolled my eyes, then said, "I'm starving! I need a snack first."

I opened a cupboard and got down crackers and a plate. I went to the refrigerator and took out the milk and some peanut butter. Then I got a knife from the drawer and spread peanut butter on my crackers. My dog, Pudgy, stared at every move I made.

As I carried my plate to the table, Pudgy leaped up and bumped my arm. Splat! A cracker landed on the floor. Pudgy gobbled it up.

After I poured my milk, there wasn't much left. I wrote a note for Dad to get more. Then I stuck it on the refrigerator where he would see it.

Finally, I could enjoy my tasty snack.

Now I really had to buckle down and do my homework. I looked around like a detective searching for clues. Where would I find examples of forces? Suddenly, it was like a light bulb went on over my head! In a flash, my homework was done.

When I showed it to my dad, he said he'd have to start calling me Gumshoe instead of Gumdrop. He had to explain to me that a gumshoe is a detective.

I think I like my new name!

FORCES

Muscles to Pull	Muscles to Push	Magnets to Pull	Gravity to Pull
- I pulled the cupboard door to open it. - I pulled the drawer to open it. - I pulled the fridge door to open it.	- I pushed the drawer to close it. - I pushed the fridge door to close it. - Pudgy pushed my arm.	- The fridge door uses magnets to stay closed. - I used a magnet to stick a note on the fridge.	- My cracker fell to the floor! - When Pudgy jumped up, gravity pulled him back down again.

CHART BY FLORA

Reflect on

Writer's Craft: Find three places where the writer used exciting words to make her voice strong.

Connections: What do you do when you have a hard time getting started on your homework?

Text Features: Photos and Captions

Photos and captions are text features that add interest to an article. They can also help you understand what you are reading.

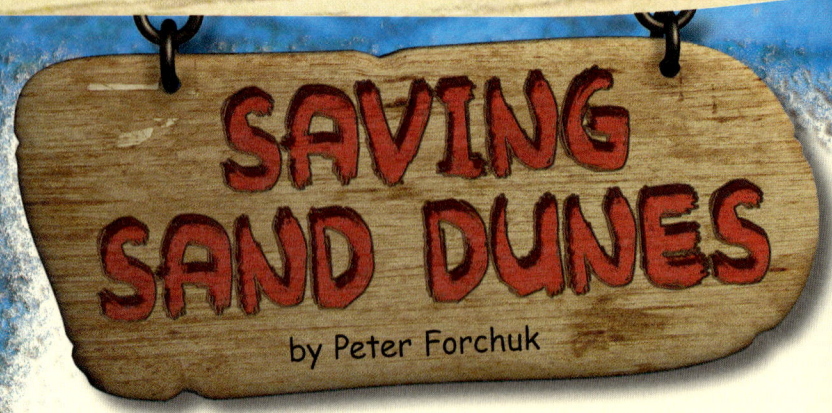

SAVING SAND DUNES

by Peter Forchuk

What Is a Sand Dune?

A sand dune is a hill made of sand. You often find sand dunes on beaches beside a lake or an ocean. Grasses and other plants often grow on top of a dune.

What Makes Sand Dunes?

The pulling force of wind and waves makes sand dunes. First, moving water erodes, or breaks down, rock into tiny pieces of sand. Then, waves push sand up onto a beach. Slowly, a dune starts to form.

Wind can push more sand onto the dune, making it grow taller. Over time, grasses and other plants may start to grow on a dune.

→

Photos help you understand the text. What do you learn about dunes in this photo?

Sand dunes can be small like this one, or very large.

Why Are Dunes Important?

Sand dunes are home to many plants and animals. Grasses and shrubs can grow on dunes. Some birds build their nests in the grass on dunes. Some red foxes make their homes among dunes.

Wild roses often grow on dunes.

Red foxes hunt for food on dunes.

←

A caption can give you more information about a photo. What information do the captions on this page give you?

What Are the Dangers to Dunes?

A big storm can destroy a sand dune. Each time a wave hits a dune, it pushes some of the sand back into the water. Lots of big waves can wash away the whole sand dune.

Walking on dunes can kill the plants that grow there.

People are also dangerous to sand dunes. Walking on the plants can kill them. Their roots help to keep the sand in place. Then wind doesn't blow all the sand away.

When people walk on dunes, they can also scare away the animals that live there.

A caption can explain why a photo is important. What important ideas do the captions on this page give you?

Driving over sand dunes is even worse than walking on them.

How Do People Protect Sand Dunes?

Here are some ways to protect sand dunes:

1. Put large branches or old Christmas trees on dunes. These help to stop wind from pushing sand off dunes.

2. Build wooden paths through dunes. These stop people from killing plants by walking all over dunes. Plants help to protect dunes.

3. Put up fences or signs to keep people away from dunes.

You can protect sand dunes by staying away when you see a sign like this one.

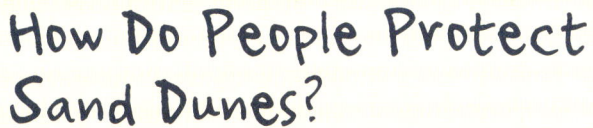

DO NOT WALK ON DUNES

←

Photos help you understand the text. How might the photo on this page help readers understand the text?

HAVE YOU SEEN WIND?

Applying Strategies

Text Features: Photos and Captions

As you read, use text features to help you understand what you are reading:

- Photos help you understand the text.

- A caption can explain why a photo is important.

- A caption can give you more information about a photo.

Wind is moving air. Wind can push things. Have you ever felt the wind pushing you? A strong wind can push you over!

We cannot see wind, but we can see what wind does. Take a look at some of the things wind can do.

Wind can make waves. Strong winds make big waves.

Wind makes windmills turn. Windmills can make power for us.

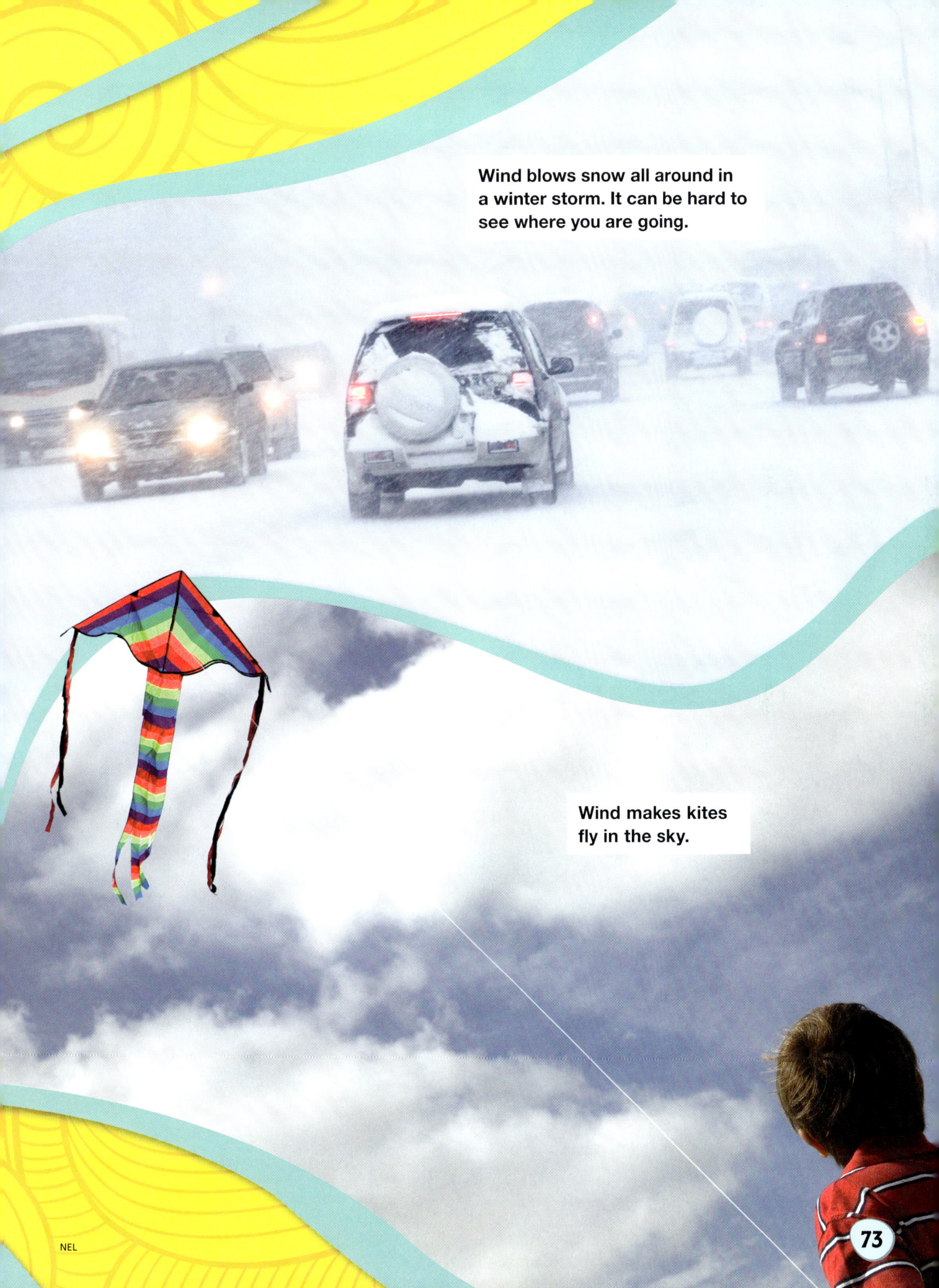

Wind blows snow all around in a winter storm. It can be hard to see where you are going.

Wind makes kites fly in the sky.

Wind can make you run after your hat.

Wind takes hot-air balloons to places far away.

Sometimes wind helps us. Sometimes wind makes problems for us.

What kinds of things have you seen wind do?

Reflect on

Strategies: How did photos and captions help you understand what you were reading?

Connections: When has wind helped you? When has wind made problems for you?

Look Out Below!

by Beth MacInnes

Applying Strategies

Text Features: Photos and Captions

As you read, use text features to help you understand what you are reading:

- Photos help you understand the text.

- A caption can explain why a photo is important.

- A caption can give you more information about a photo.

What Is a Landslide?

It starts high up the mountain. You hear a low rumbling sound. Soon, there is a loud roar as soil and stones come sliding down. Watch out for the landslide!

Gravity can pull soil, rocks, and plants down the side of a hill or mountain. People call this a landslide.

Some landslides creep very slowly down mountains. The most dangerous ones crash to the bottom in just seconds!

Soil from this landslide buried houses.

DANGER! LANDSLIDE AREA

What Causes Landslides?

Many things can cause landslides. Too much rain or melting snow may make the soil very wet. Then, gravity pulls the wet soil down the mountain.

Rivers can cause landslides. The force of moving water can wear away the soil near the bottom of a hill. This may make the soil that is higher up begin to slide down.

People may cause landslides when they are building on mountains. Heavy machines can shake the soil and make it loose. Then, gravity makes it slide down.

This landslide in British Columbia tore down trees.

Why Are Landslides Dangerous?

People and animals can be hurt or killed by landslides. The pushing force of moving soil may knock down forests. A landslide can wreck roads and train tracks.

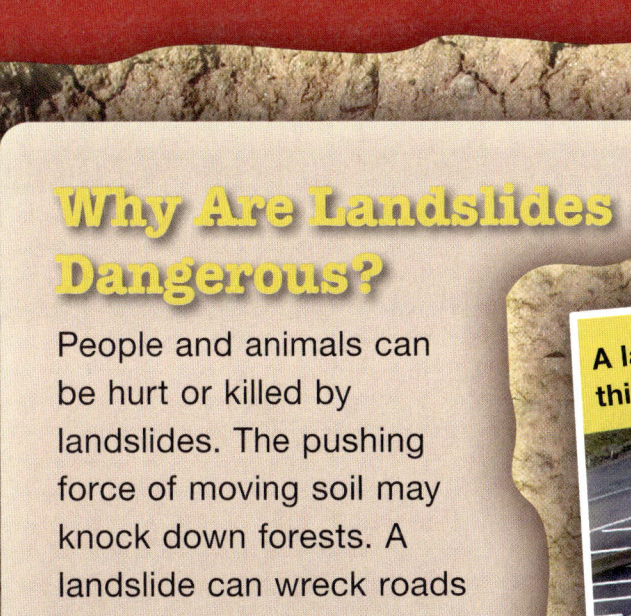

A landslide broke up this highway.

What Can People Do?

In some places, people plant trees so landslides won't happen. Tree roots hold on to the soil. Then gravity cannot make the soil slide down.

Sometimes, people put up signs in places where landslides may happen. If you see one of these signs, stay safe and stay away!

Planting trees on a mountain can prevent landslides.

Reflect on

Strategies: How did captions help you understand what was important about the photos in this article?

Your Learning: How could knowing about forces be helpful to you on a camping trip in the mountains?

Listen to Me!

Recognizing Different Points of View in Presentations

Classmates can tell you their opinions, or points of view, in presentations. Often, they hope to convince you to share their points of view. Recognizing different points of view will help you learn new things and do your own thinking.

Imagine you are listening to this student's presentation.

Listen to find out what the speaker thinks or feels about the topic. What is this speaker's topic? How does he feel about the topic?

Listen for reasons why the speaker thinks or feels this way. Why does this speaker think it's important to have the windmills?

Try to think of different points of view on the topic. Who might have a different point of view from this speaker? What might that person say?

SAY YES TO WINDMILLS!

We should all support the plan to put windmills beside Westside Park! Windmills are a great way to make energy. There are other ways to make energy. But some of these ways put pollution into the air. Windmills don't pollute.

The hill beside Westside Park is perfect for windmills. There is lots of wind there. People don't live close by, so they won't hear any noise that the windmills make.

I think windmills are beautiful, and they help keep our air clean. Say yes to the windmills!

Now, imagine you are listening to this student's presentation. Listen to find out what the speaker thinks or feels, and why. What is your point of view on this topic?

NO WINDMILLS NEAR THE PARK!

Many people are upset about the plan to put four windmills on the hill beside Westside Park. We need to stop this plan!

These windmills use the force of wind to make electricity. It's good that windmills can make electricity without polluting the air. So what's the problem?

Westside Park is a beautiful place where people can go to be in nature. It is far away from the noise of cars and trucks. Windmills would spoil the view from the park. They can also be noisy. I say we should put the windmills somewhere else. Let's keep the park quiet and not spoil the view!

Asking Questions

You can learn by listening and asking questions. Asking questions helps you check your understanding. Asking questions also helps you find out about things you wonder about.

Jason's dad talked to Jason's class about the Shanghai maglev train in China. It's a super-fast train that runs on magnets.

How to ask questions:

☑ When you don't understand something, ask a question.

☑ When you want more information, ask a question.

SAFETY IN MOTION

Putting It All Together

As you read, remember to use the strategies you've learned in this unit:

- Ask questions.
- Use photos and captions to help you understand what you are reading.

How can science help you stay safe? Let the Safety Team tell you all about it!

Cast

Narrator
Joan
Miguel
Sue
Leon

NARRATOR: The Safety Team uses what they know about science to stay safe while they have fun. Listen to what they have to say.

Safety gear protects you from forces when you're on the move.

JOAN: When I roller skate, I can move fast! I wear a helmet to protect my head. If I fall, the helmet will hit the ground before my head does and take most of the force.

MIGUEL: Don't forget kneepads, elbow pads, and wrist guards. If you fall, your knees, elbows, wrists, and hands will be protected, too.

NARRATOR: The Safety Team thinks about science and safety on the playground, too.

MIGUEL: Playground swings move back and forth. I never walk in front of, or behind, a moving swing. If I did, I could get knocked over!

The force of a moving swing can knock someone over.

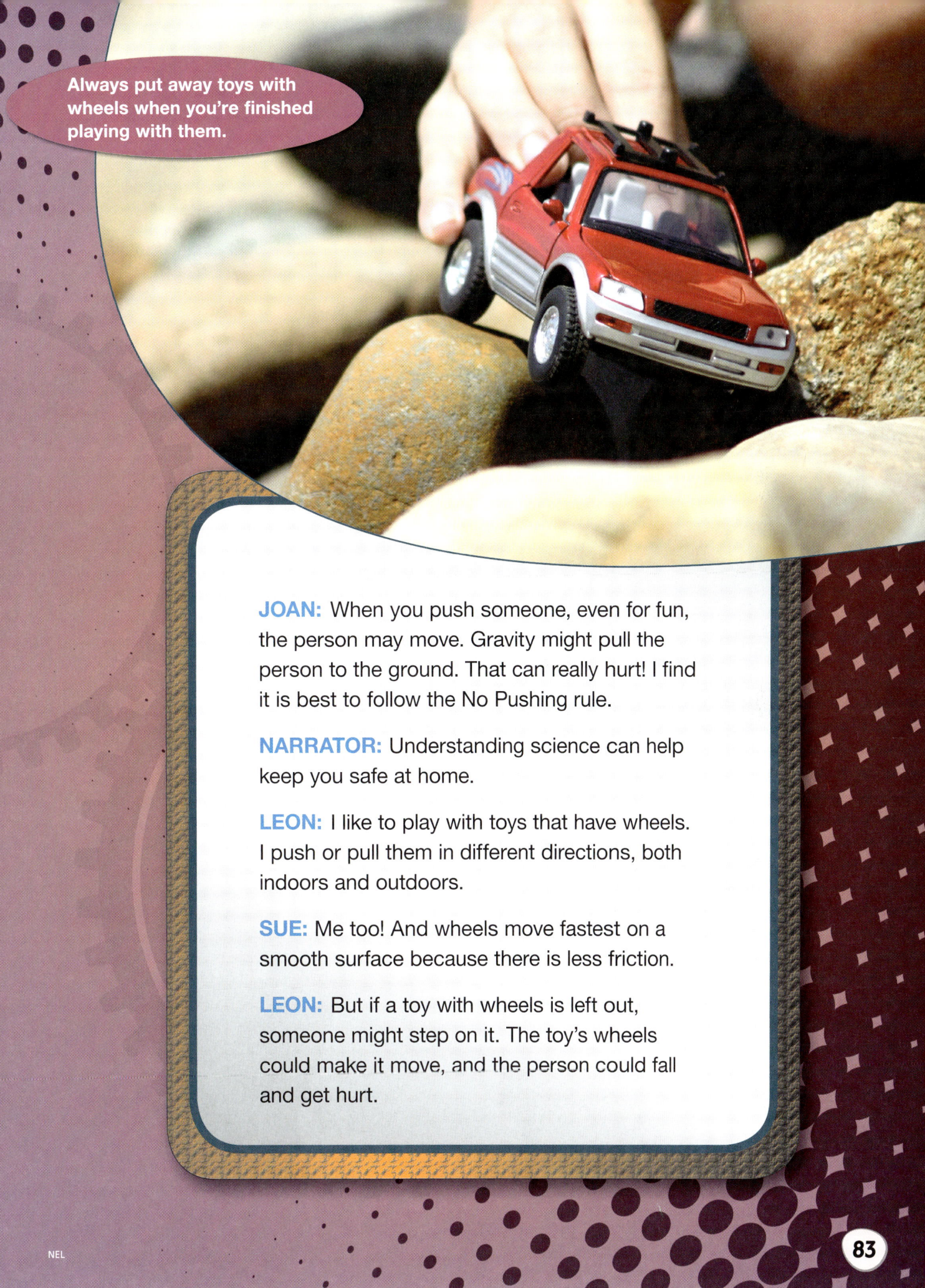

Always put away toys with wheels when you're finished playing with them.

JOAN: When you push someone, even for fun, the person may move. Gravity might pull the person to the ground. That can really hurt! I find it is best to follow the No Pushing rule.

NARRATOR: Understanding science can help keep you safe at home.

LEON: I like to play with toys that have wheels. I push or pull them in different directions, both indoors and outdoors.

SUE: Me too! And wheels move fastest on a smooth surface because there is less friction.

LEON: But if a toy with wheels is left out, someone might step on it. The toy's wheels could make it move, and the person could fall and get hurt.

SUE: So, remember to put away wheeled toys after playing with them.

NARRATOR: Science and safety matter in the car, too. In fact, they can save your life!

SUE: A moving car might stop suddenly or hit something. That force can make you move inside the car. A safety belt or car seat will protect you. Both can stop you from banging into a window or other things in the car.

NARRATOR: Time is up. We have to put on the brakes. We hope you will be part of the Safety Team.

ALL: And use science to stay safe!

The law says you must use a car seat or safety belt to protect you in a car.

Reflect on

Strategies: How did photos and captions help you understand the ideas in this selection?

Connections: What can you do to help younger children become part of the Safety Team?

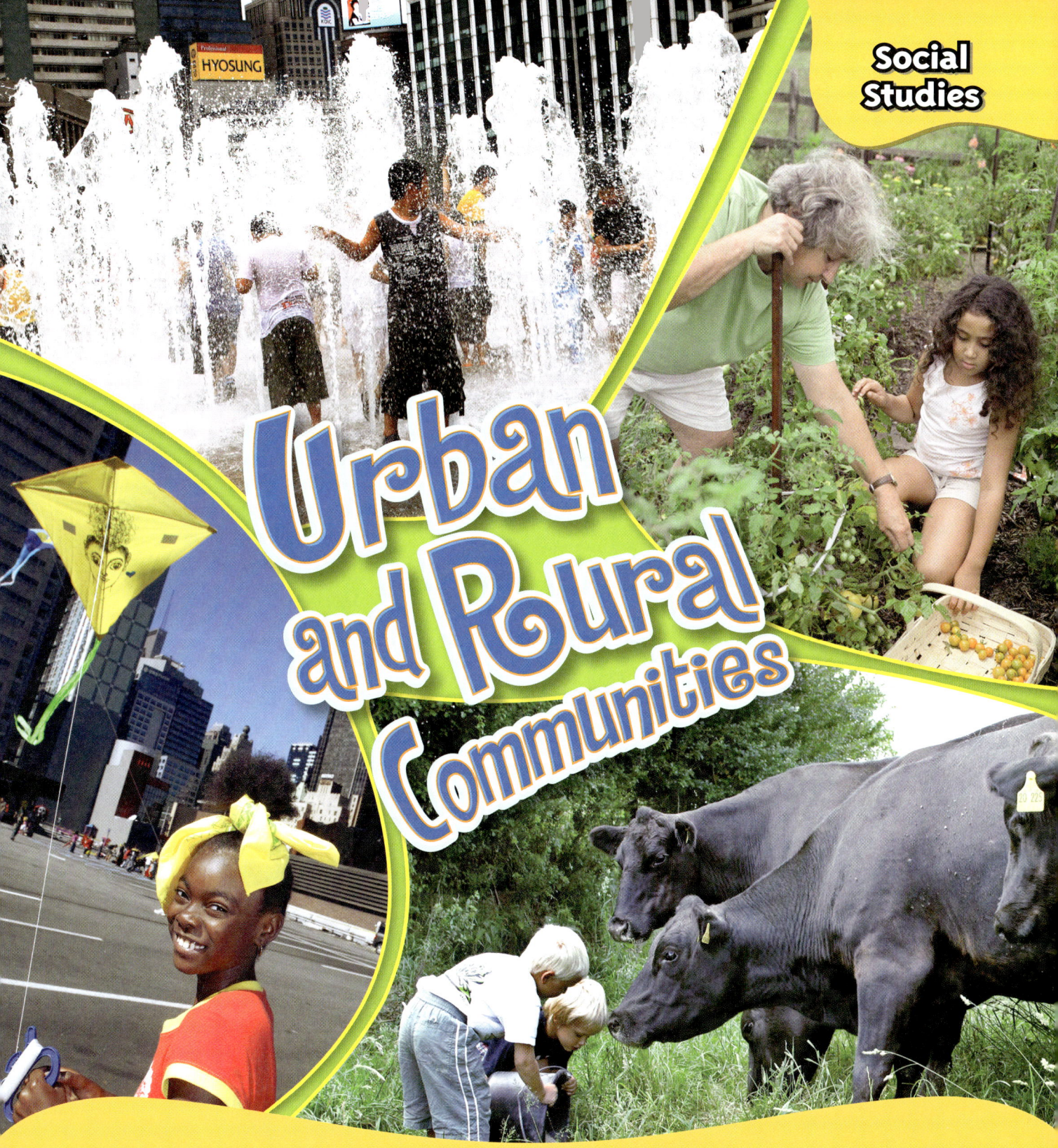

Urban and Rural Communities

In this unit, you will

- find important ideas while reading

- write words that describe

- identify important ideas while listening

- identify characteristics of sequence text pattern

- identify conventions of murals

- learn about urban and rural communities

What's That Doing There?

NEL

Look at this photo of a big city's downtown area. Some things don't belong. Can you find seven things that belong in a rural community instead?

Finding Important Ideas

Finding important ideas helps you understand what you are reading. When you think about what you have learned, you want to remember the important ideas.

Read the title and beginning lines, and then decide on a purpose for reading. What will you learn when you read this article?

Figure out how the article is organized. What are the two big sections in this article about?

Where Do

Do you live in an urban community or a rural community? How can you tell? Let's find out.

What's It Like in an Urban Community?

Many people live close together. There are different kinds of homes. There are many large and tall buildings. There are many different ways for people to get around. You might hear traffic, sirens, construction machines, and other sounds that tell you people are busy.

Housing

In cities and large towns, many people live in apartments. Some apartment buildings are very tall; some are shorter.

Some people live in townhouses and semi-detached houses. These are attached to other houses.

Some people live in houses that stand alone.

Stop at the end of each section and look for important ideas. What kinds of housing would you see in urban communities?

You Live?

Getting Around

Buses, streetcars, and trains can carry a lot of people at a time. Buses can go on any street. Streetcars run on streets that have tracks. Subway trains run underground. Light-rail trains run above ground.

Taxis can carry a few people at a time.

Some people ride bicycles and motorcycles to get around the city.

Others like to drive their own cars and trucks to get around.

Stop at the end of each section and look for important ideas. How do people get around in urban communities?

Stop at the end of each section and look for important ideas. What would you see and hear in a rural community?

What's It Like in a Rural Community?

A few people live spread out over a large area.

Small towns are rural communities with homes and some businesses. Usually, there are no really tall buildings. You might hear birds, frogs, wind, and other nature sounds because there is less "people noise."

Housing

People who live in the country live in houses with large yards or farmland around them.

Some people live in mobile homes on their own land or in a community of mobile homes.

Stop at the end of each section and look for important ideas. What kinds of housing would you see in rural communities?

In town, some people live in apartments above stores. Some towns have small apartment buildings.

Getting Around

People who live in the country or in small towns drive their own cars and trucks to get around. Some people drive snowmobiles and all-terrain vehicles (ATVs) on trails.

Children who live in rural homes take school buses to get to and from school in the nearest town.

Now you can answer the question: Do you live in an urban community or a rural community?

Wherever you live, your community is your home.

Stop at the end of each section and look for important ideas. How do people get around in rural communities?

Our Homes

Written by Jill Bever and Sheilah Currie
Illustrated by Sharon Matthews, Bernadette Lau, Lionel Drew, and Gordon Sauvé

See what these children have to say about their homes.

Cathy's Home

I'm Cathy. I live in a house near the ocean. My house is in a small fishing village. I like to watch the fishing boats go by.

Yoma's Home

I'm Yoma. This is the townhouse where I live. My best friend, Kim, lives right next door. Our townhouses are attached.

Julie's Home

I'm Julie. My family lives on a farm. We live in the house. The animals live in the barn. We all like to be outdoors.

Jamal's Home

I'm Jamal. I live in an apartment in the city. We have a swimming pool in our building. There is a park nearby to play in.

Tom's Home

I'm Tom. I live in a house on a reserve. I like to paint pictures of the trees around my house.

Reflect on

Strategies: How did thinking about the way the article is organized help you find important ideas?

Your Learning: Which of the homes looks the most interesting to you? Why?

The Adventures

Written by Norma Kennedy • Illustrated by Barbara Spurll

Meet the Mice

Mort is an urban mouse. He lives in a city, where many people live close together.

Howie is a rural mouse. He lives near a small town, where there are not as many people, and they live farther apart.

Mort and Howie plan to visit each other. First, Howie travels to Mort's urban community.

It's Busy Downtown!

MORT: Welcome to my city, Howie!

HOWIE: There are so many people! Look out! We almost got stepped on!

MORT: Yes, there are lots of people here in the city.

# of Two Mice

All Kinds of Buildings

HOWIE: What are all those huge buildings?

MORT: The really tall ones are apartment buildings and office buildings. There are also stores, banks, and restaurants on this block. There are lots of other buildings, too. Isn't it great?

HOWIE: I don't know. Where are the trees and grass?

MORT: Oh, there are parks, too.

Watch Out for Traffic!

MORT: Come on! Let's get some food over there.

HOWIE: But there's too much traffic—buses, streetcars, cars and trucks, and bicycles!

MORT: I know! Later I'll show you the subway train. It runs underground.

HOWIE: How will we get across the street?

MORT: Just stick close to me. I'll get you there safely!

Eat and Run

MORT: Cheese, biscuits, popcorn, and cookies. All my favourites!

HOWIE: Ooohhh, my poor tummy! I've never had this kind of food. Where does it all come from?

MORT: There are many different kinds of restaurants around here. We never run out of food.

MORT: Oops! We'd better get out of here! Here comes the garbage truck!

HOWIE: What? What's happening? I can hardly move! Oh! I'm moving! I'm moving!

The Countryside

HOWIE: Now you'll see what it's like to live away from the city. This is a town.

MORT: Where are the tall buildings? Why aren't there a zillion people rushing around?

HOWIE: Towns have fewer people than cities. Many of the people have lived here all their lives. They take time to chat with each other as they go around town. This town has most of the same kinds of buildings as your city has. They're just smaller. Look how much sky you can see!

MORT: There's not much traffic.

HOWIE: People in small towns don't need buses, streetcars, and subways to get around. Most of them drive or walk. Listen to the quiet! Smell the fresh air!

Watch Out for Cows!

MORT: Hey! I've seen buses like that in the city!

HOWIE: Here, they take the kids who live outside of town to school and home again. Here's where I live.

MORT: Eek! What are those monsters?

HOWIE: Don't worry about them. Cows won't bother you. But they do share some yummy food! Follow me into the barn. Try some of this tasty grain.

MORT: Oh! This doesn't taste like food! Where is the cheese? Don't you have any cookies?

HOWIE: Come on! Let's see what we can find to eat out in the field.

NEL

Eat and Jump

HOWIE: Try some of this fresh …

MORT: Howie! What's that noise? Look! There's something coming after us!

HOWIE: Oh, that's the tractor. Just jump out of its way.

So Long!

MORT: Thanks for showing me life in the country, Howie. Now I'm going back to the city, where there's good food and lots going on all the time. And no cows or tractors!

HOWIE: Thanks for showing me life in the city, Mort. I'm staying here in the country, where there's good food, lots of space, and fresh air. But let's visit again sometime!

Reflect on

Strategies: How did reading the title and beginning lines help you decide on a purpose for reading?

Critical Literacy: Imagine that both mice wrote about life in the city. How would their articles be the same and different?

Jason's Journey

Written by Jessica Pegis
Illustrated by Renée Benoit

Applying Strategies

Finding Important Ideas

As you read, look for important ideas to help you understand and remember what you are reading:

- Read the title and beginning lines, and then decide on a purpose for reading.

- Figure out how the article is organized.

- Stop at the end of each section and look for important ideas.

Big News

"Hey, Jason," called Dad. "You know that great place we go every summer, with the subway and all those tall buildings you love to look at? Well, we're moving there."

Jason slumped in his chair.

"We're moving to the city, to Grandpa's house," said Mom.

"I know it's a big change, Jason, but you're going to love it there," said Dad. "There are things to do in a big city that you can't do anywhere else."

"I wish we could just stay here!" Jason said angrily.

Goodbye, Hometown

Jason walked to the main street of town.

Stony Ridge was a small town on a large lake. From where he sat, Jason could see most of the other buildings—the general store, the post office, the plumbing supply store, the bakery, and the tackle shop where his dad worked.

Stony Ridge was a quiet place in winter, but in the summer, thousands of cottagers came to the area. As he walked home, he thought glumly about what it would be like to live in a place with three million other people.

Goodbye, Farm

The next morning, Jason went to visit Gran on her farm. Gran still grew all her own fruits and vegetables.

"I hear you're moving to the city," Gran said.

"Yeah," Jason sighed. "I don't want to move."

"Why don't you want to move?" Gran asked.

"Because it's going to be noisy and crowded and you can't see any stars at night," said Jason. He sounded angry.

"Well, you'll be living close to downtown," Gran said. "Within 20 minutes, you can be at a swimming pool, or a baseball game, or a museum, or a movie theatre. You can travel around by subway, bus, or streetcar."

"I remember the museum," said Jason. "They had a great dinosaur exhibit."

"That's right," said Gran. "Give the city a chance."

Hello, City

The day of the move finally arrived. It was time to get in the car for the drive to the city.

At first, the highway had only two lanes. Then, it became wider. Jason counted eight lanes of traffic. The number of cars seemed to have tripled, and all of them were going very fast.

Now, lots of large, low buildings appeared.

"Are those factories?" Jason asked.

"Some of them are," said Dad. "Some are offices, and some are warehouses. Okay, folks. We're almost there!"

The downtown buildings seemed enormous. They were all different sizes and shapes. Most were covered with glass.

"Are we going to live close to those buildings?" Jason asked.

"Those are office towers, and we sure are," said Dad. "If you walk to the end of our street, you'll be able to see the whole downtown from across the park."

"Can we do that tonight, Dad?"

"Of course," Dad chuckled.

Feeling at Home

Now Jason could see his new neighbourhood. The buildings were very close together. There were cars parked on both sides of the road. The sidewalks were crowded with people.

Finally, they pulled up to his grandfather's house. Jason thought about going to the swimming pool, a movie theatre, a baseball game, and the museum. He thought about riding the subway and streetcars. He started to feel better about the move.

"Dad, let's take that walk after the sun sets," Jason said. "I want to see the city all lit up at night."

His dad winked at him and said, "It's a deal."

Reflect on

Strategies: How did stopping at the end of each section help you find the important ideas?

Connections: What other stories about boys and girls moving to new homes have you read? How were these stories like Jason's story?

Using Words to Describe

When you want to tell someone what something is like, you describe it. The words you choose help readers make pictures in their minds.

This writer is describing the park near her house. She chooses words that describe what she could see, hear, feel, and smell when she was there.

MY PARK

The park is a busy _{and beautiful} place. <del>Kids go</del> ^{Toddlers splash} in the wading pool.

Kids <del>play</del> ^{shout, swing, climb, and slide} on the playground. People <del>talk</del> ^{chat} and read _{newspapers}.

Tall trees give shade and flowers smell sweet. <del>It's pretty</del>.

How to use words to describe:

☑ **Picture in your mind what you want to describe.**

☑ **Choose words that tell what you see, hear, feel, and smell.**

☑ **Read your writing out loud. Ask yourself, "Will my words help readers make a picture in their minds?"**

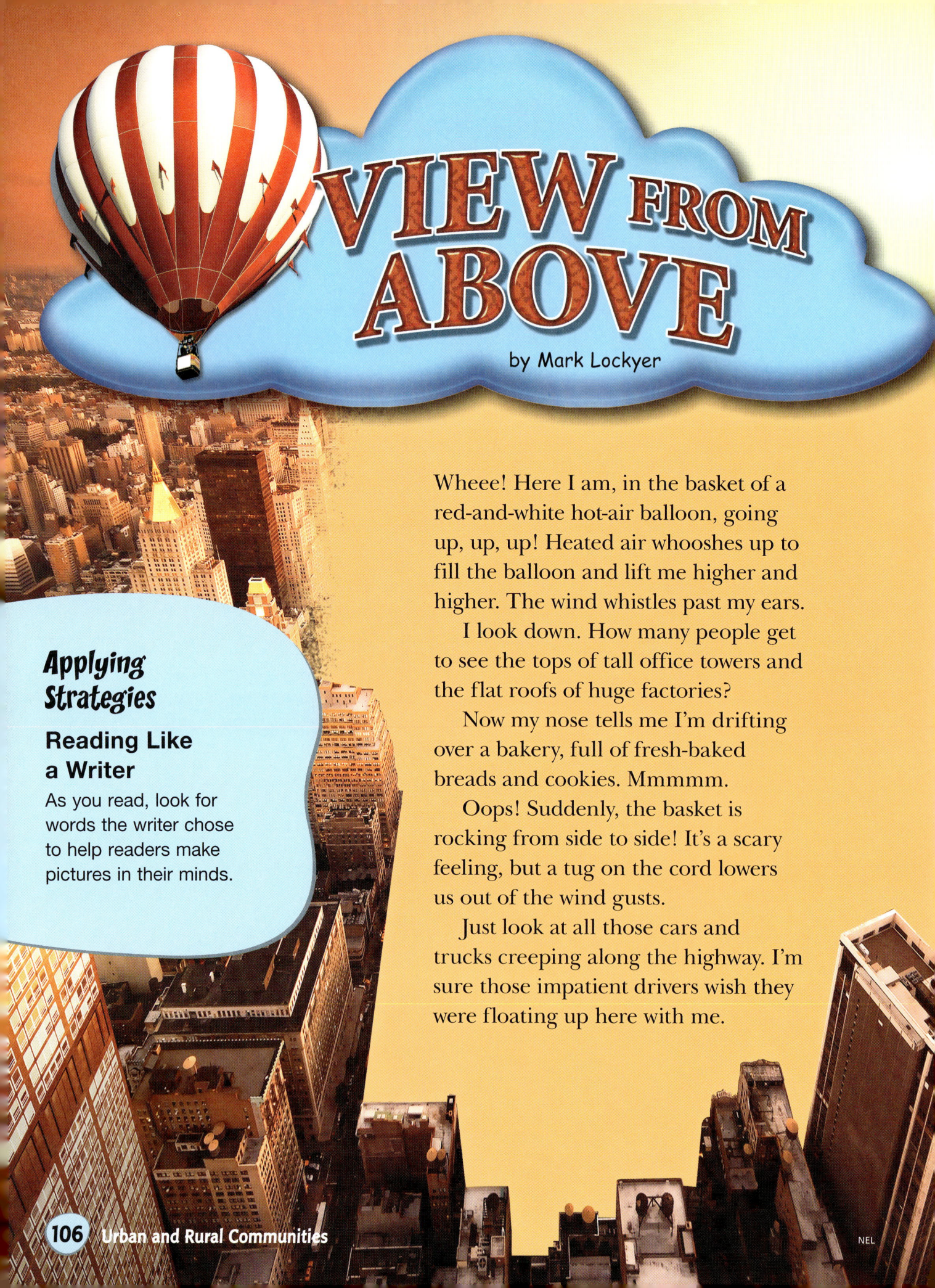

VIEW FROM ABOVE

by Mark Lockyer

Wheee! Here I am, in the basket of a red-and-white hot-air balloon, going up, up, up! Heated air whooshes up to fill the balloon and lift me higher and higher. The wind whistles past my ears.

I look down. How many people get to see the tops of tall office towers and the flat roofs of huge factories?

Now my nose tells me I'm drifting over a bakery, full of fresh-baked breads and cookies. Mmmmm.

Oops! Suddenly, the basket is rocking from side to side! It's a scary feeling, but a tug on the cord lowers us out of the wind gusts.

Just look at all those cars and trucks creeping along the highway. I'm sure those impatient drivers wish they were floating up here with me.

Wow! Outside of the city is a different view—fields of new crops, trees with shiny new leaves, and grassy parkland. So much *green*!

I squint at a wiggly line in the distance. Oh, now I see that it's a river. It cuts a zigzag path through the land.

The river rushes through a small town. Friendly people wave at me. I make the balloon dip and waggle. That's *my* kind of wave!

Then, with a big grin, I lean over and shout down, "I love to fly!"

Reflect on

Writer's Craft: Find three words or phrases that helped you make pictures in your mind.

Connections: When have you looked down from a high place? Describe what you saw.

Identifying Characteristics of Sequence Text Pattern

Writers use sequence text pattern to show the order in which things happen.

Use text features, like headings and photographs, to help you identify the sequence. Read the title and first heading. What is the order, or sequence, of events in this article?

Look for time words to help you understand the order of events. Which words show you the order of events in springtime?

FARMING
THROUGH THE SEASONS
by Virginia Schomp

In the Spring

It's springtime on the farm. For many farmers, spring is the beginning of the growing season.

First, the farmer ploughs the field. Sharp blades bite into the ground, breaking up the hard soil. Next, the tractor tows the seed drill. Up and down the field, the drill pokes holes into the ground and drops in seeds. Soon, neat rows of tiny plants will pop their heads above the ground.

The tractor pulls the seed drill that plants the seeds.

In the Summer

After they've sprouted, plants need food to keep growing. The farmer makes the soil richer by adding fertilizer. Soon after being fertilized, the plants put on a growth spurt!

Growing plants must be protected. Early in the summer, chemicals are sprayed on fields to kill weeds, insects, and diseases.

Growing plants need water, but not too much. Too much rain could cause flooding. Too little rain could turn green fields brown.

Sometimes, farmers have to water dry fields. Pipes and sprinklers carry the water from streams and holding tanks to thirsty crops.

These irrigation sprinklers turn like the hands of a clock.

Use text features, like headings and photographs, to help you identify the sequence. Read the heading on this page. Predict the next two headings.

←

Look for time words to help you understand the order of events. What happens first, fertilizing the plants or protecting the plants with chemicals?

Look for time words to help you understand the order of events. What is the important event in the fall?

→

In the Fall

After a summer of growing, crops are ready for harvesting. Some crops are picked by hand. Most are harvested by machines.

A combine harvests wheat, corn, and other grain crops. At the same time, it separates the grain from the rest of the plant.

The combine pours the cut grain into the wagon pulled by the tractor.

Look for time words to help you understand the order of events. What happens to crops after they're harvested?

→

After they're harvested, some of the crops are sold. Some are stored to feed the farm animals through the winter.

In the Winter

During the winter, the farmer feeds hay and grain to the farm animals, and gives them extra straw to keep them warm in the barn.

When the animals have been taken care of, the farmer cleans and repairs tools and machines.

All must be ready for the start of a new growing season.

In winter, farm animals need the farmer's help to get food.

Look for time words to help you understand the order of events. When does the farmer clean and repair tools and machines?

←

milk on the

by Doyle Cooke

Where did that cold, fresh milk come from?

It came from the store. But how did it get to the store?

It started at a place like this. This is a dairy farm. Many cows live here. The farmer takes good care of them.

The cows are milked two times a day, every single day. Milking machines make the farmer's work easier. The milk is stored in big containers.

1

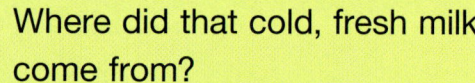

2

MOOVE

③

Next, the milk is loaded into a tanker truck. It keeps the milk cold and clean.

Where is the milk going?

The truck takes the milk to a factory. The milk is treated to make it safe to drink. Then it is made into different kinds of milk and other dairy products.

④

After that, bags and cartons of milk are loaded onto another truck. This truck also keeps the milk cold as it travels.

Where is the milk going now?

The truck delivers the milk to stores. Stores put the milk on shelves that keep it cold. Then people buy it.

Finally, people take the milk home and put it in the refrigerator.

The next time you have a glass of cold, fresh milk, think about how it travelled from the dairy farm, to the factory, to the store, and then to your glass!

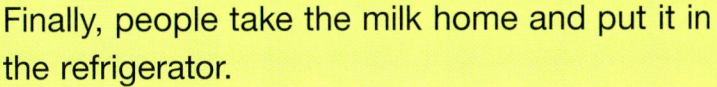

Reflect on

Strategies: What text features helped you identify the sequence of events in this article?

Connections: How many things in your refrigerator started with the milk from a cow on a dairy farm?

My Visit to Iqaluit

Farouk Khan

My family likes to visit Canada's capital cities. This year, we went to Iqaluit (ee-ka-loo-eet). It is the capital of Nunavut. It's way up in northern Canada. You can't get there by car. You have to take a plane.

Here is my journal of our visit.

Day 1

our first look at Iqaluit

Today we flew into Iqaluit! There are no trees and no other cities around. Dad said the land is tundra. Tundra stays frozen all year long!

After we landed, we took a taxi to our hotel.

Day 2

We walked around town today. The streets were busy with cars and trucks. In winter, many people get around on snowmobiles.

We saw some beautiful buildings. I liked the school that looks like blocks of ice.

Nakasuk School

The grocery store had fresh fruits and vegetables. Mom said the prices were pretty high. That's because they come from so far away. You can't grow vegetables on tundra!

We carried our map everywhere!

Day 3

We got up early. Then we rode on ATVs to a big park outside of town. The lake water was so-o-o clear. We could see Arctic char swimming around. That's a kind of fish. Fishers catch them and eat them at home or sell them to restaurants. People can eat the fish fresh or dried.

In the morning, we hiked around parts of the park. There were waterfalls and all kinds of birds. Then we stopped and had our picnic lunch. After lunch, we sat by the water and joked about going for a swim. Brrrrr! After a snack beside the lake, we rode our ATVs back to our hotel.

drying strips of fish on the line

the chilly water of Sylvia Grinnell Lake

Day 4

Today we went to the Visitor Centre. There were sculptures, paintings, beadwork, carvings, weavings, clothing, and jewellery to look at and to buy. Mom bought a carving of a polar bear. It's carved out of soapstone.

"David of the North" is carved out of one piece of marble!

a carver working with soapstone

After lunch, we had a helicopter ride. It was very exciting! We flew over land and water. We saw flowers and birds and muskox. I even saw a walrus.

Tonight, I had Arctic char for dinner. It was delicious!

It was a super last day of our visit to Iqaluit!

a young walrus

Reflect on

Strategies: What time words helped you understand the order of events in Day 3 of the writer's visit?

Your Learning: If you were planning a trip to Iqaluit, what places would you like to see?

Look Again!

Identifying Conventions of Murals

Imagine you are walking down a street you know. Suddenly, you're passing by a farm that looks as real as your running shoes. What happened? You spotted a mural.

A mural is a large picture painted on a wall. What clues do you have that this mural was painted on an outdoor wall?

Murals look very realistic because they use a technique called perspective. Perspective is the art of making flat images look real. What part of this mural would make you stop and look?

Murals make town and city walls exciting. How might this wall have looked before the mural was painted?

Would this mural attract your attention?
Why or why not?

Identifying Important Ideas While Listening

Teachers and other leaders often tell you things you need to know. Learning how to identify important ideas while listening will help you understand and remember what you hear.

[Comic panels:]

WE'RE ALMOST THERE. LET'S REVIEW OUR SAFETY RULES.

MR. ARCH IS TALKING ABOUT SAFETY. BETTER LISTEN!

THE MUSEUM WILL BE CROWDED. KEEP YOUR PARENT LEADER IN SIGHT AND STAY WITH YOUR GROUP.

WATCH MRS. WILSON.

STICK TOGETHER.

YOU ARE NOT PERMITTED TO EXPLORE OUTSIDE!

STAY INSIDE!

REMEMBER! STAY IN YOUR GROUP. WATCH YOUR LEADER. DO NOT LEAVE THE MUSUEM.

I CAN DO THAT!

How to identify important ideas while listening:

☑ **Make sure you know the speaker's topic.**

☑ **Pay attention to the speaker's tone of voice and gestures.**

☑ **Listen to see if the speaker repeats important ideas in his or her conclusion.**

ARE WE THERE YET?

Written by Paula Lee • Illustrated by Rob Fiore

I'm so excited! We're on our way to our favourite vacation place. I hear the car's engine chugging; I feel the car moving forward. Even though I am blind, my ears, nose, and skin tell me about each part of our trip. Come along for the ride, and I'll show you!

PART 1: THROUGH THE CITY

The first part of our trip takes us through the city. I open my window so I can hear and smell and feel where we are. We stop and go, stop and go. Truck engines rumble noisily. We creep through heavy downtown traffic. The aroma of grilled hot dogs reaches my nose. A block later, the smell of spicy Chinese food makes my mouth water.

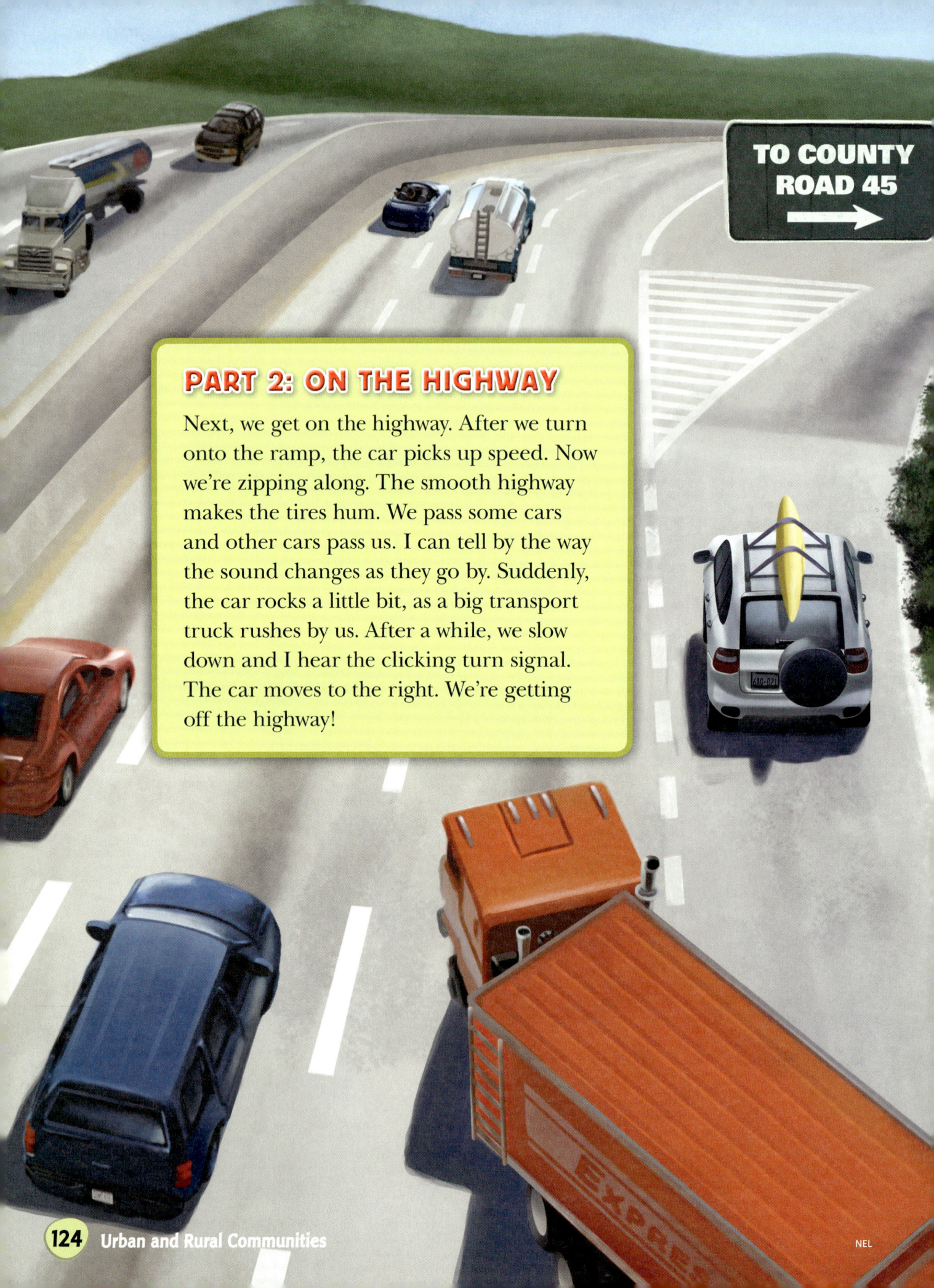

TO COUNTY ROAD 45 →

PART 2: ON THE HIGHWAY

Next, we get on the highway. After we turn onto the ramp, the car picks up speed. Now we're zipping along. The smooth highway makes the tires hum. We pass some cars and other cars pass us. I can tell by the way the sound changes as they go by. Suddenly, the car rocks a little bit, as a big transport truck rushes by us. After a while, we slow down and I hear the clicking turn signal. The car moves to the right. We're getting off the highway!

PART 3: IN THE COUNTRY

After we get off the highway, we drive more slowly. The road is bumpy. The smell and feel of dust tells me we're on a dry gravel road. Instead of cars and trucks, I hear the "Caw! Caw!" of a crow and the singsong chirping of other birds.

Eeew! There's a really strong smell coming through the window! A tractor rumbles by close to the road. I wonder what that stinky stuff is that the farmer is spreading on the fields.

Suddenly, the car slows and stops. Mom says that a duck and her ducklings are crossing the road. How I wish I could feel their feathery softness!

PART 4: HERE AT LAST!

After two more stops and three turns, I hear the harsh calls of gulls. Then I smell the water and plants and other things that live in and near the water. The car rolls to a stop. The lapping of the waves makes me hurry to get outside.

The very next minute, grainy sand sticks to my bare feet as my sister and I skip down to the water's edge.

This is the very best part of the whole trip! We're here—at our special vacation place!

Reflect on

Strategies: How does the writer use sequence text pattern to help you enjoy the family's drive?

Critical Literacy: How might this story be different if the narrator could see?

Credits

This page constitutes an extension of the copyright page. We have made every effort to trace the ownership of all copyrighted material and to secure permission from copyright holders. In the event of any question arising as to the use of any material, we will be pleased to make the necessary corrections in future printings. Thanks are due to the following authors, publishers, and agents for permission to use the material indicated.

Text

10-12: *Green Cat* © 2002 by the Estate of Dayal Kaur Khalsa is published by Tundra Books. **15-17:** "Mrs. Murphy and Mrs. Murphy's Kids" from *Jelly Belly* by Dennis Lee (Macmillan of Canada, 1983; Key Porter, 2001). Copyright (c) 1983 Dennis Lee. With permission of the author. **20-22:** Adapted extract from the original text *WHAT! CRIED GRANNY* by Kate Lum, and illustrations by Adrian Johnson, altered by Nelson for this use. Used with permission of the publishers Bloomsbury Publishing Plc and Penguin Young Readers Group, a Member of Penguin Group USA. **23-26:** From *He Came With the Couch* (c) 2005 by David Slonim. Used with permission of Chronicle Books LLC, San Francisco. Visit ChronicleBooks.com **27-32:** *Amos's Sweater* Copyright © 1998 by Janet Lunn. First published in Canada by Groundwood Books Ltd. Reprinted by permission of the publisher. **33-35:** Text and illustrations used with the permission of Orca Book Publishers. **37-40:** From *The Day Jimmy's Boa Ate the Wash,* text copyright (c) 1980 by Trinka Hakes Noble, artwork copyright (c) 1980 by Steven Kellogg. Used by permission of Dial Books for Young Readers, A Division of Penguin Young Readers Group, A Member of Penguin Group (USA) Inc., 345 Hudson Street, New York, NY 10014. All rights reserved. **42-46:** Text and illustrations used with the permission of Orca Book Publishers. **50-53:** Material from *Move It! Motion, Forces and You!* written by Adrienne Mason is used by permission of Kids Can Press Ltd., Toronto. Text (c) 2005 Adrienne Mason. **60-63:** From HOUGHTON MIFFLIN SCIENCE, Level 2 by Valentino et al. Copyright (c) 2007 by Houghton Mifflin Company. Reprinted by permission of Houghton Mifflin Harcourt Publishing Company. **All rights reserved. 81-84:** From HOUGHTON MIFFLIN SCIENCE, Level 2 by Valentino et al. Copyright (c) 2007 by Houghton Mifflin Company. Reprinted by permission of Houghton Mifflin Harcourt Publishing Company. All rights reserved. **92-93:** From Currie/Bever. *INFOREAD SS 1: Our Homes,* 1E. (c) 2003 Nelson Education Ltd. Reproduced by permission. **100-104:** From *INFOREAD SS 3: Community Stories Book 4.* 1E. (c) 2004 Nelson Education Ltd. Reproduced by permission. **108-111:** Reprinted from *If You Were a Farmer,* by Virginia Schomp with permission from Marshall Cavendish.

Photos

Cover: (clockwise) © Randy Faris/Corbis; From Mechanimals by Chris Tougas. Used with the permission of Orca Book Publishers; Matthew Jacques/Shutterstock. **5:** dani92026/Shutterstock. **7:** Tony Metaxas/Asia Images/Getty Images. **18:** Garfield (c) 2008 Paws, Inc. Reprinted with permission of Universal Press Syndicate. All rights reserved. **19:** Foxtrot (c) 2007 Bill Amend. Reprinted with permission of Universal Press Syndicate. All rights reserved. **27-32:** Adam Gryko/Shutterstock. **46:** Matt Houser/Shutterstock. **41:** Corbis/Jupiter Images **57-59:** (background) Christopher Dodge/Shutterstock; (background) Domen Colja/Shutterstock; (background) Laurent Renault/Shutterstock. **60-63:** (background) Tischenko Irina/Shutterstock. **60:** (c) HMCo./Richard Hutchings Photography. From HOUGHTON MIFFLIN SCIENCE, Level 2 by Valentino et al. Copyright (c) 2007 by Houghton Mifflin Company. Reprinted by permission of Houghton Mifflin Harcourt Publishing Company. All rights reserved. **61:** (c) HMCo./Ken Karp Photography; (c) HMCo./Richard Hutchings Photography. From HOUGHTON MIFFLIN SCIENCE, Level 2 by Valentino et al. Copyright (c) 2007 by Houghton Mifflin Company. Reprinted by permission of Houghton Mifflin Harcourt Publishing Company. All rights reserved. **62:** (top) (c) HMCo./Ken Karp Photography. From HOUGHTON MIFFLIN SCIENCE, Level 2 by Valentino et al. Copyright (c) 2007 by Houghton Mifflin Company. Reprinted by permission of Houghton Mifflin Harcourt Publishing Company. All rights reserved. **63:** (c) HMCo./Ken Karp Photography; (c) HMCo./Richard Hutchings Photography. From HOUGHTON MIFFLIN SCIENCE, Level 2 by

Valentino et al. Copyright (c) 2007 by Houghton Mifflin Company. Reprinted by permission of Houghton Mifflin Harcourt Publishing Company. All rights reserved. **68-71:** (background) a_ Taiga/iStockphoto. **68:** (top to bottom) frentusha/iStockphoto; Marko Heuver/Shutterstock. **69:** (top to bottom) © aaron peterson.net/Alamy; David Wrigglesworth/Oxford Scientific/ Jupiter Images. **70:** (top to bottom) Fitzer/iStockphotos; Mike Powell/Riser/Getty Images. **71:** © M. Timothy O'Keefe/Alamy. **72-74:** (background) North Design/Shutterstock. **72:** (left to right) Rafa Irusta/Shutterstock; © Horizon International Images Limited/Alamy. **73:** (top to bottom) Igumnova Irina/Shutterstock; RTimages/Shutterstock. **74:** (top to bottom) Soren Hald/Stone/Getty Images; dani92026/Shutterstock. **75-77:** (background) tadija/iStockphotos. **75:** AP Photo/La Prensa Grafica, FILE. **76:** (c) REX/CP Images. **77:** (top to bottom) AP Photo/Bjrn Larsson Rosvall,Scanpix; David Frazier/Stone/Getty Images. **81-84:** (background) Milushkina Anastasiya/Shutterstock. **81:** Al Bello/Getty Images. **82:** © JUPITERIMAGES/ Thinkstock/Alamy. **83:** lovleah/iStockphotos. **84:** (c) Dylan Ellis/Corbis. **85:** (clockwise) Thomas Nord/Shutterstock; James Baigrie/FoodPix/Jupiter Images; © blickwinkel/Alamy; © Richard Levine/Alamy. **86-87:** (background) Hisham Ibrahim/Photographer's Choice/ Getty Images. **86:** (left to right) Bjorn Heller/Shutterstock; luchschen/Shutterstock; Ariusz Nawrocki/Shutterstock. **87:** (left to right) Neil Webster/Shutterstock; Kurt De Bruyn/ Shutterstock; inacio pires/Shutterstock; Stephanie Davis/Shutterstock. **88:** (top to bottom) Sergey Lazarev/Shutterstock; jamalludin/Shutterstock; Panoramic Images/Getty Images. **89:** (top to bottom) Sergey Lazarev/Shutterstock; © Bert Klassen/Alamy; © ClassicStock/ Alamy; Timur Kulgarin/Shutterstock. **90:** (clockwise) © Richard Cummins/Corbis; Walter Bibikow/Stone/Getty Images; Denise Kappa/Shutterstock. **91:** (clockwise) © Chad Ehlers/ Alamy; © Daniel Dempster Photography/Alamy; Aron Brand/Shutterstock. **94:** (top to bottom) kwest/Shutterstock; emin kuliyev/Shutterstock. **95:** Natalia Bratslavsky/Shutterstock; Tom Antos/Shutterstock; niderlander/Shutterstock. **96:** (top to bottom) R. Gino Santa Maria/Shutterstock; fckncg/Shutterstock; kenny1/Shutterstock. **97:** Michael Shake/ Shutterstock; track5 /iStockphoto; Len Green/Shutterstock; dem10/iStockphoto; Andrey Karataev/Shutterstock. **98:** (top to bottom) Sharon Meredith/Shutterstock; Lisa F. Young/ Shutterstock; Pchemyan Georgiy/Shutterstock; Matthew Jacques/Shutterstock; mortenklevis iStockphoto. **99:** (top to bottom) ownway/iStockphoto; Ragnar Schmuck/fStop/Getty Images; Noam Armonn/Shutterstock; Mikael Damkier/Shutterstock. **100-104:**(background) Dariusz Gudowicz/Shutterstock; (background) Sharon D/Shutterstock. **106:** Jim Parkin/ Shutterstock; Ilja Ma'ïk/Shutterstock. **107:** fotoVoyager/iStockphoto. **108-111:** (background) Noam Armonn/Shutterstock; (crates) GeoffBlack/iStockphoto; (icons) browndogstudios /iStockphoto. **108:** Vasina Natalia/Shutterstock; © George Impey / Alamy. **109:** Sarah McHattie/Shutterstock; © David Frazier/Corbis. **110:** GeoffBlack/iStockphoto; © Agripicture Images/Alamy. **111:** (c) Eastcott/Momatiuk/The Image Works. **112:** (top to bottom) Eric Gevaert/Shutterstock; Laila Kazakevica/Shutterstock; Graeme Norways/Stone/Getty Images. **113:** (top to bottom) Robert Pernell/Shutterstock; David R. Frazier/Photoresearchers/ First Light. **114:** (c) Dick Hemingway Editorial Photographs. **115:** George Doyle/Stockbyte/ Getty Images. **116-119:** (background) Peter Jochems/Shutterstock; pdtnc/Shutterstock. **116:** CP PHOTO/Jeff McIntosh. **117:** © Sean O'Neill/Alamy. **118:** CP PHOTO/Fred Chartrand; © Alison Wright/CORBIS. **119:** (clockwise) RENE JOHNSTON/Toronto Star; CARLO ALLEGRI/AFP/Getty Images; Corbis/Jupiter Images. **120-121:** (c) Charles Weiss Art Studio

Illustrations

4: Mike Laughhead; **5:** Barbara Spurll; **8–9:** illustrated by Gary Locke; **13–14:** illustrated by Mike Laughhead; **15–17:** illustrated by Scott Burroughs; **36:** illustrated by Jason Bone; **41:** illustrated by Steve Manale; **48–49:** illustrated by Jason Bone; **50–53:** illustrated by Anton Petrov; **54–56:** illustrated by Ron Berg; **57–59:** illustrated by Dean Klevin; **64:** illustrated by Steve Manale; **65–67:** illustrated by Matt Roussel; **78–79:** illustrated by Brian Mclachlan; **80:** illustrated by James Yamasaki; **92:** (top to bottom) (c) Sharon Matthews; (c) Bernadette Lau. **93:** (top to bottom) (c) Sharon Matthews; Gordon Sauve/Three in a Box; Lionel Drew/Three in a Box. **94–99:** illustrated by Barbara Spurll; **100-104:** (c) Renne Benoit; **105:** illustrated by Brian Mclachlan; **116 and 117:** illustrated by Scott Ritchie; **122:** illustrated by James Yamasaki; **123–126:** illustrated by Rob Fiore